I0642090

Charles Godfrey Leland

The Art of Conversation

With Directions for Self Education

Charles Godfrey Leland

The Art of Conversation
With Directions for Self Education

ISBN/EAN: 9783337811372

Printed in Europe, USA, Canada, Australia, Japan

Cover: Foto ©Thomas Meinert / pixelio.de

More available books at **www.hansebooks.com**

ART OF CONVERSATION,

WITH

DIRECTIONS FOR SELF EDUCATION

NEW YORK:

Carleton, Publisher, Madison Square.

LONDON: S. LOW, SON & CO.

M DCCC LXX.

Entered according to Act of Congress, in the year 1864, by

GEO. W. CARLETON.

In the Clerk's Office of the District Court of the Southern District of
New York.

CONTENTS.

PREFACE.

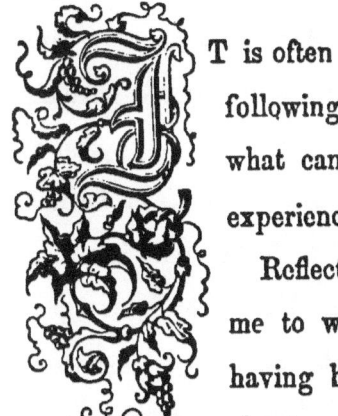

T is often urged against works like the following, that they profess to teach what can only be acquired by practical experience.

Reflection over this objection induced me to write the ensuing pages. And having borne it in mind through every chapter, I trust I may be pardoned for dissenting from such a canon of criticism. Conversation is like chemistry, something which must of course *result* in actual practice, but it is as true of the one as of the other, that it is based on comprehensible facts which may be set forth in books.

The truth is, that this objection is a relic of the old school, which jealously restricted all familiarity with the elegant arts of life to a favored few, whose interest it was to create the impression that such arts were veiled by a mystery never to be comprehended by the multitude. This impression was enforced by identifying good-breeding, accomplishments and grace, with innumerable frivolous laws of etiquette, and by making the whole depend on intimate acquaintance with the fleeting *mode* or fashion, which was however attainable in perfection only in a court circle. It is however worth remarking, that a very great proportion of this elegance of the old school " which no books can teach," was entirely derived from dancing masters and teachers of " style " — themselves members of that lower class of society above which their pupils, thanks to their efforts, were to be so mysteriously exalted.

There has been of late years a great change in the opinions of the world regarding etiquette and elegance, since the dancing master has been dethroned, and the master of ceremonies no longer takes precedence of the school-teacher, clergyman and editor. Social intercourse, even in royal circles, is every day being based more and more on the laws of common sense, of kindness and of respect for the innate dignity of every man, than on the accidents of rank, and on a conventional, Japanese-like etiquette. The laws which lend grace and a charm to life are, in other words, becoming more distinctly intelli gib.e, and more capable of being defined as something real, even in a book.

Not only within the past fifty years, but actually dur ing the present decade, have there been striking changes in the manners of gentlemen, and in the tone of conver- sation, as regards laying aside an affected and silly eti- quette for the natural dictates of the heart, and for a so- cial code which treats the poorest man as a gentleman, so long as he behaves like one. Republicanism is, in fact, becoming the law among the most highly cultivated, while the worn-out frippery of the old school is, oddly enough, cherished principally by the wealthy and am- bitious vulgar.

That the spirit of the conversation of the present day is infinitely more capable of being presented in a book than was that of the old school will, I imagine, be denied by no one who is impartially familiar with both. And such readers will, I trust, give their sympathy to a very sincere effort which the author earnestly hopes will not be without effect in disseminating among the young men of America some knowledge of the refinements of social intercourse as based upon manliness, common sense, in- tellectual culture, and a kindly regard for the rights of others, instead of the scraps of an artificial and shallow etiquette which is rapidly·becoming a matter of ridicule.

I should state in connection with this subject, that an additional impulse to write this volume was given by ex amination of a number of current works on society, conversation and etiquette. The tone of nearly all seemed so singularly old fashioned, so frivolous and imitative of merely superficial "manners," that it was with real concern I learned that such books are sold annually in incredible numbers. That their effect must be to make silly fops, instead of brave-hearted and truly cultivated gentlemen, is apparent on every page. One very popular work tells its reader of "A little book entitled 'The Art of Tying the Cravat,' which is as indispensable to a gentleman as an ice at twelve o'clock." A very recent volume — and by far the most pretentious of them all — declares that our conduct in society should consist of "a happy medium between well-directed insolence," and "the subordinating our own vanity to the vanity of others." Another work of sober·tone consists chiefly of hackneyed moral axioms, and tends to make the great law of social intercourse an anxious care to abstain from everything like amusement or cheerfulness — its hero of a diary being a youth who. regretted he had not worked hard on the Fourth of July! Another deals principally in such arts as retiring gracefully from a room, "which can only be done by an easy *side-step*, accompanied by a graceful bow" — a performance which the author de-clares is very difficult, and requires much private prac-tice, but which is indispensable, "since *nothing* is so rude and *disgusting*, as to turn your back upon any one." The same writer, while urging the advantages of what he terms "female conversation," adds as a climax to the disasters which must result from neglecting such conver-sation, that should you do so, "you will certainly never learn *to dress*" — this *dressing*, be it observed, consti-tuting a very important part of his manual of politeness.

I should be indeed sorry to refer in such a manner to the writings of others were they simply *harmless;* but such coxcomb's doctrines are not harmless, since they make great mischief, in common with all that pretends to teach young people that. true culture is a matter of bows, expense, elaborate toilettes and grimaces ; or on the other hand that it consists of sad austerity instead of genial kindness, intellectual culture, joyous appreciation of all that is merry and wise, and of life as it should be among either rich or poor.

The object of this book is therefore briefly as follows :

There is a strong 'tendency in the present age to base the laws of social intercourse upon a standard of dignity and of rights common to all, and to treat every one as a gentleman and an equal, so long as he behaves civilly. To do this, common sense teaches us that we must tacitly lay aside most of that *artificial manner* which a poor man, however courteous he may be by nature, cannot be expected to have learned. It is on this ground that I would establish the principles of conversation and of culture.

The reader will readily understand that I do not mean that a gentleman should at *any* time forget his natural ease, grace, or correct language. I refer simply to that indefinable annoyance, that expressive exaction of a servile deference, which was as marked in the gentlemen of the old school as their shoulder-knots, diamond buttons and swords, and which is still common in the more provincial English nobility and their institutions.

As regards the rules for self-instruction in literature, I would state that having during many years past frequently commended them to persons whose education has been partly neglected, and having witnessed in several cases results beyond my expectations, I have been induced to give the hints in question a place in this volume, with the sincere hope that their efficacy, in which I have that faith which results from experience, may be generally tested.

It is the application of the principle of beginning with a few leading facts, of adding to them day by day, of constantly reviewing what has been learned, of assiduously combining and working up into new forms all the knowledge thus gained, and, in short, of developing the memory of the whole by association, which forms the method of teaching languages, so successfully followed by the pupils of OLLENDORFF and of AHN. My effort in these pages has been to indicate the plan by which this system may be practically applied to the acquisition not merely of a language, but of any other branch or branches of learning.

It may have occurred to the reader, that the manner in which foreign writers have found fault with the social peculiarities of the American people involves in reality a high compliment, since in judging of the conduct of the mass in this country, they invariably adopt as their standard that of the *first* class in their own nation. It would be preposterous to compare the majority of our citizens to the peasants of Europe, and a knowledge of the facts involved proclaims that moral and intellectual culture is constantly making rapid advances in every division of society among us. Progress in all things, and above all things in advancing the dignity of labor, is in the United States no hackneyed axiom, but a great and living *truth*, which most men take warmly to heart, and in which they live and have their being. In this truth, thousands, as I now write, are risking their lives, and for it thousands of lives will yet be offered — all to advance the sum total of human happiness.

In the great system of social culture which occupies so prominent a place in that of progress, the arts of freely communicating our thoughts, and of acquiring knowledge, are anything but insignificant. If by the publication of a few chapters, most sincerely written in the hope of doing good, and which I trust are not entirely without some basis of observation and study, I shall succeed in aiding though but a little, those arts, my most earnest ambition will be fully realized.

THE AUTHOR.

INTRODUCTION

HERE is no social art in which it is so generally desirable to excel, as in Conversation.

The man or woman who can fulfil all the conditions of talking well, has at command a means of success which, when directed by common sense, is fully equal to all the advantages afforded by birth and fortune combined. With it the woman of moderate personal attractions can draw around her admirers, while the mere beauty remains a wall-flower.

Wealth and rank often lose their charms to the possessor, and even the exercise of accomplishments at times grows wearisome. But the pleasure of well-sustained social intercourse always retains its zest. We love power; and of all power the most agreeable is that which comes from personal influence. It is for this reason that kings and other very eminent persons so often excel in conversation, and astonish the world by their happy faculty of adapting themselves to the most varied natures. They soon grow weary of the flattery addressed merely to their rank, and therefore devote themselves to the art of personally pleasing, or of impressing those whom they meet. And as they receive full encouragement and have every social advantage, they seldom fail to make rapid progress. George the Third has been greatly ridiculed as regarded his personal peculiarities, and yet it would be difficult to point out in any literature the report of a conversation so happily combining sense, courtesy, tact and wit, as that which he he.d with Doctor Johnson, as we find it narrated by the latter.

But it is not necessary to be a king to talk well, except so far as acquiring control over the kingdom of our mind is concerned. Every one who will devote himself to the art can acquire in it a degree of skill which will ensure respect in any society. By practising dancing you learn to dance with ease; and by studying all the resources of conversation and by putting them in practice as often as opportunity occurs, you will end by talking well under the most trying circumstances, acquiring ease of manner and self-possession among those whose presence would otherwise be to you oppressive.

Conversation cannot be entirely learned from books, but books are quite capable of giving information, and of making suggestions which every lady or gentleman of ordinary intelligence can turn to good account in this art, and thereby acquire very great advantages. The author was acquainted with a gentleman of wide experience in society, who was noted for his agreeable conversation; and for this he owed much, as he confessed, to reading what had been written on the subject. No one will deny that the difference between well-bred and vulgar children, is in a great measure due to the precepts of parents; and yet all of those precepts may be given in black and white. If the reader who is conscious of any deficiency as regards the ability to appear to advantage in society, will set himself to work in good earnest to remedy his defects, even with no other teacher than a book, he may be confident of success

But to ensure it he must labor diligently. *Nil sine labore* — nothing without labor. Rules and examples should be borne in mind and assiduously followed at all times.

There is at least one great advantage in acquiring this very useful art — its practice demands no loss of time. On the contrary, when properly applied it saves time. Those who converse correctly, invariably induce others to talk more intelligibly with them, and such people even in making bargains, come more distinctly to terms. Every time the student speaks to any one, he may turn his knowledge to advantage. The porter at the street corner, the sailor lounging in the sun, the elegant lady with whom you exchange a few fleeting words in greeting; your servant, your principal, your officer, your friend, may all be made to aid in your mental culture and to *feel it* — so soon as you by pains and perseverance begin to realize that you are acquiring it. Nay, the most powerful minds can be led in any direction you will, as an elephant may be baited here and there by a child with a few grains of rice, if you choose to simply introduce or *lead* the subjects which pertain to the direction required. Rules — even rules in books — can be made of the greatest possible utility in these respects.

Language is the reflection of morals and manners, of the life and of the heart. He who endeavors to correct his conversation will also endeavor to correct the defects which control it. In leaving off abusive expressions one learns to cure the habit of *thinking* evil of others and of gloating over their faults — for after all said, the " hypocrites " who play such a part in old fashioned dramas — the men who use language to conceal their thoughts — have become rare in this age, because they succeed in deceiving very few. Many may fancy themselves adepts in the art of disguising their characters, but the vulgar, yet expressive, word " humbug " seldom fails to be commonly applied to them.

No man ever gave himself in earnest for any great length of time to the object of succeeding in the art of conversation, and of thereby making himself generally acceptable in society, without ridding himself of many defects, which if not positive vices, at least had nothing in common with goodness. To converse *well* is to acquire that delicate morality of the heart which leads on the one hand to kindness, and is on the other mysteriously allied to good taste in matters of life, of literature and of art. — Hence it will be found that in those circles where a very high standard of social intercourse is exacted, and which is expressed and tested by excellence in conversation, genius is most readily freed from the clogs of prejudice, of suspicion and of vulgarity, and quickly manifests itself in great works. Talents are nowhere so rapidly developed as among people who in their intercourse aim at constant elegance and propriety in discourse or discussion, and this latter is not the result, but rather the *cause* of the development. It has often been a matter of wonder that great minds are more generally developed in groups, than singly; in cities than in the country. No one doubts that the same Anglo Saxon blood exists all over America or England, with the same average of talent; and in every corner of the two countries may be found highly educated men. But how much greater is the proportion of genius which is developed into actual results by social intercourse than by solitary reflection! The real reason for it is, that now and then a circle is formed whose mem‑bers cultivate the art of mutual expression and of mutual intelligence — in other words *the art of conversation* — and thereby succeed in a short time in imparting to each other not merely a general knowledge of what they themselves know, but also

what they themselves *are*.   Among men and women
who consciously or unconsciously excel in conversation, experiences of travel and of adventure, of personal intercourse with eminent characters, and impressions of remarkable objects, are communicated
with a vividness which no written description can
convey.   Tones, gestures, glances, attitudes and
smiles supply a *color*, so to speak, remaining indelibly
impressed upon the memory, and which no book can
ever impart.   A single reminiscence of Lord Byron,
narrated by an accomplished " conversationalist,"
has made upon my mind an impression far more viv-
id, and which seemed to give a deeper insight to the
personality of the poet, than did all of Lady Bles-
sington's written experiences.

It will therefore be readily understood, that people
of ability greatly increase that ability, and enable
one another to produce great works, not merely by
mutually meeting, but by cultivating the art of conversation so that they may give and take knowledge
to the greatest possible advantage.   As regards the
pleasure to be derived from the proper exercise of
the power which this art bestows, little need be said.
One person, and especially any one accomplished woman, who excels in it, is enough to cast an air of

cheerfulness over a whole *soirée;* to sustain for weeks a spirit of gayety at the dullest watering-place; to draw together in any society and then draw *out* the best qualities of every one to advantage, to unite congenial minds which would otherwise have remained unknown to each other, and in fact to exert a genial influence as of sunshine in all places and at all times. It is usual to attribute such power entirely to "disposition" or to natural "gifts." Much is of course due in these happy instances to ability or to "advantages," but I am firmly convinced from observation, that after all it is chiefly owing to the expansion which is given by judicious cultivation of the art of conversation. The world is full of men and women of kindly feelings, and even of excellent educations, who have indeed every requisite to not only achieve social eminence but to elevate others with them — "if they only know how" — that is to say, if they could only impart their thoughts, sentiments or moods, with ease and tact, to others.

It may not be in the power of any writer to render every reader to this degree accomplished. But it is very possible that the reader may by perseverance do as much for himself; and I shall have succeeded in my object, should I be so fortunate as to induce any into whose hands this book may fall, and who may be conscious of a need of instruction as regards the subject of which it treats, to strive to remedy the defect.

CHAPTER I.

ATTENTION IN CONVERSATION.

HE best talkers are the best listen-ers " is an axiom which has been repeated, in one form or the oth-er, in every cultivated language. " The duty of paying attention to what other people say is a funda-mental law of the social code." You may be able to startle with your wit, move by your pathos, and thrill with your eloquence — but all this will not save you from being frequently a positive annoyance unless you have occasionally what Sidney Smith de-sired in a loquacious gentleman — a few flashes of silence.

The duller the intellect and the more limited the

knowledge and experience may be of the person with whom you talk, the more will he wish to hear himself, and the less will he desire to listen to you, save for applause and flattery. Bear patiently with such people, and content yourself with following the example of SIR WALTER SCOTT, by directing their conversation to subjects on which they can give you useful information. Remember that there are few persons from whom you cannot learn something, and that everything is worth knowing.

Whenever you meet with a man or woman who seems disposed, as the French say, to defray all the expenses of the conversation, you would do well to become a listener and limit yourself to an occasional remark, which you will have time to render piquant, and which, if apropos, will make the greater impression on your " subject." Patience is the first of all social virtues, but Silence is her most useful handmaid. And though you be even a JOB by nature, you will seldom take part in a conversation in which the two may not aid you. I can safely say, that in reviewing my own studies of conversation I find that those who produced the most favorable impression on all, were men or women who indicated the possession of great patience. No degree

of brilliancy or of knowledge will impress well
bred people with a sense of superiority at all com-
parable to that which is awakened by patience and
self-command.   It is the true basis of the *savoir
faire*, or "knowing how to act correctly under all
circumstances," which is the whole art of being a
man of the world.

It would be well if every one would once a day
reflect on the proverb which states that we seldom get
into trouble by saying too little, but very often by
saying too much.

There is an inexpressible courtesy and a true nobility in deference and in attention when paid by
children to parents ; by young girls or ladies to any
who are older than themselves, or by young men to
any one.   It indicates a very high degree of culture
and refinement, and is an unfailing omen of success
in life.   But it becomes far more beautiful and
noble when manifested by either old or young towards inferiors.   Many people excel in courteously
evading or getting rid of the conversation of others,
but the lady or gentleman has mastered a much
higher grade in the "art of living" who can listen
with interest to all, especially to the poor and humble, without manifesting impatience, indifference or
affectation of interest.

While silent in conversation and while listening, never stare away to the right or left, and be careful to avoid all appearance of inattention or of abstractedness. Look steadily at the speaker — if he or she be a person of sense it will be an admonition to be concise, for it is not kind to compel prolonged attention from those who are so courteous as to bestow it.

A French writer has however, ingeniously observed that one is justifiable in seeming to be inattentive or in a reverie when praised by another, or when a flattering allusion is in any way made to an action, a work or a remark which does him honor.

To attend to many persons, or to look steadily at them may require modifications. I have seen women as well as men who to whatever might be uttered, not excepting the lightest jests, never varied from a steady stare which seemed to say, "I will know the whole truth — you cannot deceive me." No rudeness was intended, but the impression which the stare gave was that of a want of courtesy. One may look steadily and yet politely.

To recur to my text, let the reader never forget in any conversation, under any circumstances, that

it is not only the best part of courtesy, but also of
policy to be rather a listener than a speaker. Pol-
hymnia, the muse of Eloquence herself is repre
sented with a fore-finger on her lip to signify that
silence if aptly employed sets off language to the
best advantage.

CHAPTER II.

OF INSPIRING CONFIDENCE IN CONVERSATION.

 REQUISITE element of agreeable conversation is that it be unrestrained, and to do this you must inspire confidence in your discretion.

Strive by every means in your power to avoid the reputation of a tattler. Never repeat to a soul a syllable which was not intended for repetition. Make it a point of personal pride to be reserved on this subject.

Few persons seem to be aware of the advantages which are to be derived from having the character of never repeating anything that is told them. Most people in the warmth of conversation say much which

they trust will be kept secret, and quite as many, it
may be added, repeat nearly all of these confidences,
hoping that an injunction to secrecy will protect
them from all consequences. How can they hope
that others will be more truthful than themselves ?

But those who are truly faithful in their reserve
enjoy an advantage, as regards making friends, which
it is difficult to exaggerate. With many women, the
mere conviction of such a merit in a man is enough
to insure intimacy and unreserved confidence. He
who hopes to become a favorite with the fair sex cannot begin too soon, or labor too assiduously, in creating the impression that the most trivial secret.
whether imparted to him or acquired by accident, is,
in his keeping, perfectly safe. But it will be vain
to attempt to gain this character unless it be founded *in fact.* A single bit of gossip in circulation
stamped with your name, will excite general distrust
and doubt as to your fidelity. If you can establish
a character *with yourself* for secrecy, others will
soon elevate it to something remarkable.

The whole world is full of people craving for confidence — people to whom a secret is like gold in a
child's pocket, burning to be issued. Those who are
high in rank and blessed with every advantage are

often tormented for want of "a true friend;" meaning thereby some one to whom they can confide secrets. And on those who will simply take them
and *keep* them, they are willing to bestow friendship.
To those who would be in such confidence it is
enough that they follow the advice already given of
never being directly or indirectly the means of disseminating gossip of any kind.

In connection with this subject I may properly
advise the reader against *curiosity.* There are people who cannot see a letter without craving to know
to whom it is addressed, or who cannot find anything written lying on a table, without involuntarily
picking it up. The Paul Pry is the meanest character of society, and he who would feel superior in
strength and in integrity should strive vigorously
to have nothing in common with such a type of base-
ness.

———

Bear continually in mind the fact that in the art
of conversation the secret of success lies not so
much in knowing what to say, as in what to avoid
saying.

Every man or woman of ordinary intelligence can

by resolutely acquiring information and imparting it in correct language, become a good talker. But to become a good conversationalist, it is necessary to influence the minds of others. You must establish a genial and sympathetic tone between yourself and the one with whom you discourse, so that in the end your friend may retain the conviction that *he* has said nothing which sober second thought would disapprove, or to which you would recur with doubt. To do this is always in the power of either. It consists in following rigorously the simple rule:

"Those please most who offend the least."

It is not enough to refrain in conversation from annoying those who are present, or from censuring the absent. It is extremely characteristic of a gentleman or lady to abstain from *all* gossip whatever or from meddling reference to other people and their affairs. I am aware of the very great difficulty of determining what is, or is not, proper to be discussed of other people. Many things *must* be known, and of many others that knowledge which at one time seems impertinent, at another proves to be proper and profitable. The most sensible people not unfrequently show themselves gratified at learning that you are not ignorant of matters in relation to them, which, strictly speaking, it is none of your business to know. And a knowledge of the good or bad fortunes of those whom you encounter may have a serious influence in determining the character of your intercourse.

All of this, and much more, may be adduced by those who defend the practice of gossiping. Yet it remains true that, after all, those who least indulge in such meddling meanness are the least seldom entangled in troubles through ignorance. —To be able to resolutely avoid listening to comments on the family affairs, intentions, or mistakes of other people, requires not only firmness but *tact*, and the one who is possessed of this will seldom be involved in difficulties resulting from avoiding gossip. The lady or gentleman who can successfully achieve such a triumph will at once assume a high position as regards understanding and. threading the entanglements of life and of society. It may not be clear to the youthful reader *why* this should be so, but if he or she will implicitly follow the rule of strictly avoiding all gossip whatever, the time will come when the immense advantages gained from such observance will be as a bright light over a whole life time.

And while on this subject I may appropriately ob-

3*

serve its connection with an accomplishment of very great importance, which is generally regarded as being entirely a natural gift. I refer to *tact;* to that judicious employment of our powers just at the right time, which is so useful in life. And with it I may also mention that happy exercise of wisdom by which one is enabled to avoid those embarrassments into which the young are especially liable to fall.

It is the want of these gifts which the inexperienced in life contemplate with most dread. Let them console themselves with the reflection, that the most certain means of acquiring them is to very strictly adhere to the rule of doing as you would be done by at all times, and on all occasions, firmly resisting all temptation to the contrary. This, with the cultivation of knowledge, and of such arts of society, and accomplishments, as you can master, will be certain to impart, in time, that firmness and confidence which, when allied to grace, invariably bestow tact and practical wisdom.

I trust that the reader will not regard these remarks as the mere commonplaces of morality. They are matters of sound common sense and their application gives the best possible basis for forming an elegant man or woman of the world, of the type which is now becoming most admired and respected. At this day society is rapidly undergoing great changes. Drinking and gambling and extravagance are no longer encouraged in respectable circles as they were in the days of the gentlemen of the old school, and the heartless maxims of Chesterfield are now studied only in that second class, which always unconsciously occupies a position far behind the true leaders. I know that the young are still generally under the impression that brilliancy in society, elegance and grace in manner and in conversation, have nothing in common with love for all mankind, with forgiving our enemies, and with endeavoring assiduously to do good in every way to old and young, rich and poor. I know that it is too often believed that tenderness of heart and conscience are not to be reconciled with the character of a gay man or woman of the world, with fashion and cosmopolite style. But it is a great error, so very great that I know that all of these latter fascinations may be *best* acquired with the aid of a good heart. It is time the ridiculous error were dissipated — that one must needs be more or less hardened and frivolous to enjoy life in its most elegant phases   The truth is, that the really *best* people in the world ought to be among those who best know it — and there is no reason why they should not occupy such a position.

I trust that the reader who is desirous of excelling in conversation will peruse this chapter more than once. Should he or she succeed in thoroughly extirpating the habit of which it treats, I might perhaps conclude with this page — so confident am I that one so much purified at heart would through life meet with every social encouragement frcm all whose good opinion would be worth having.

CHAPTER III.

PERSONAL APPEARANCE. DRESS. ORNAMENTS.

Dress well; but moderate

N a well known French work on conversation, the first three chapters are
devoted to the teeth, the mouth, and
the tongue.   To those who would
excel in the art, the suggestion may
not however be amiss that as regards
personal appearance there should be
neither striking defects nor effects.
Not only should the *teeth*, as the
French writer suggests, be kept scrupulously neat,
and with them the minutest details of the entire
person, but the hair and dress should be strictly
within the average limits of the fashion of the day.
The reason for this is manifest — there should be
nothing to distract the eye or divert the attention

from the expression of he countenance, or from the words of the person conversing. The slightest neglect of cleanliness is quite enough, with the majority of refined people, to mingle a feeling of disgust with the most favorable impressions, even though they may be quite unconscious of the source of the disagreeable feeling — for such defects often open to us, we know not why, a long train of offensive associations. Neat toilettes and good clothes are to be commended, since they are in a certain sense a compliment to all with whom you associate. But for a man, jewelry and striking ornaments, gay colors and all that *attracts* the eye form serious drawbacks. People of experience in the world, especially intelligent and shrewd women, are prompt to form conclusions from foppish eccentricities of dress, which are seldom to the credit of the wearer; and though they may pay a tribute of admiration to the ornaments in themselves, it will always be discounted from the respect due to the mind of the one who bears them.

It is far safer to trust to an old coat, than to rely on the slightest neglect of neatness escaping observation.

Cheap imitative elegance is invariably vulgar, and indicates the mere fac-simile of what is in itself at

best little better than ornamental barbarism. It is
well set forth by *Punch :*

> ' Believe me if all these ridiculous charms
>   Which I see on thy watch-guard to-day,
> Were to-morrow locked up in the pawn-broker's arms,
>   Some trifling advance to repay,
> Thou wouldst still be the snob which this moment thou art,
>   Let thy vanity think what it will;
> For those shining red buttons, that breast-pin so smart,
>   And those studs, show vulgarity still ! ''

I am perfectly aware that with many men the tendency to gaudy color and display is irrepressible.
Perhaps it is well that such is the case, since it is a
matter of some importance that the weak-minded
should be promptly known whenever met, and we
may therefore regard the tendency as equivalent to
the wise provision of Nature by which we are enabled to distinguish parrots and macaws from the birds
of pleasanter temper and song.

A lady being asked what opinion she had formed
of the conversation of a certain young gentleman,
replied : " Do not ask *me !* I can remember
nothing of it all but a horrible great red coral ball
on his cravat, which rolled against all my ideas and
knocked them down like nine-pins ! ''

CHAPTER IV.

OF SATIRE, SARCASM, AND TEASING.

NEVER say anything unpleasant when it can by any possibility be avoided.

It is to be regretted that witty satire and keen retorts are so generally relished. Many persons seem to be under the impression that without sarcasm social intercourse must of necessity be dull. It is indeed too frequently believed that all wit must cut as well as shine. The temptations to indulge in this form of rudeness are consequently to many, irresistible. They learn that a single sarcasm or a stinging reply promptly conceived and well expressed often establishes a reputation. If they look into the past, they find that many men of letters, statesmen and artists, who would otherwise have been forgotten, still live in anecdotes which do credit to their heads, but very little to their hearts. They observe, too, that all manner of faults are corrected or punished by wit, and that people who would otherwise become social plagues, are frequently held in check by the fear of pointed ridicule.

But unfortunately very few observe the degree to which the *abuses* of witty sarcasm out-balance its benefits. A majority of all quarrels and ill-feelings spring from this source. Where impertinence is once crushed by wit, it is a hundred times goaded to insolence and revenge. In nearly all instances of "deserved castigations" by pointed repartee, it will be found they might have been avoided without a sacrifice of dignity, in some manner far more creditable to the intelligence of the one replying. And it should be borne in mind, that very few persons who have once become notorious for keen retorts fail to become positive nuisances. Having brought down with a single shot some one who is fair game, they end by setting up an "infernal machine" against the whole world.

It has been said that by strictly avoiding the

temptation to use slang, we end by discovering not only more correct, but even far more striking expressions as an equivalent. So it will be found that by refraining from satire and sarcasm, wit, far from being diminished, greatly increases its real power and value. Even when it is absolutely necessary to reply to insolence with a retort, and when the happiest form of a cutting answer promptly suggests itself, you should remember that it is always possible to retain the wit and administer the reproof in a manner which expresses your disinclination to inflict pain. Such triumphs of skill and kind-heartedness indicate a degree of nobility which deeply impresses every one whose admiration is worth winning.

It may be seriously doubted whether any person famed for frequent satirical retorts was ever at heart either a gentleman or lady. The professed " wit " grasps at his weapons as naturally as a groom in a quarrel grasps at a stable-fork. A man whose head and heart are alike cultivated may, like a gentleman, when taken unawares, seize the same implement, and with it defeat his foes; but he casts it aside when all is over, as though he regretted the necessity which compelled him to use it. It is very significant, that the lower the society, the greater is the relish for smart and tart sayings. At a certain depth of vulgarity we continually hear in conversation, efforts at satire followed by bitter recrimination and endless quarrelling. I trust that the young reader who aims at success in conversation and at thorough accomplishment, will reflect deeply on this subject. He cannot fail to ascertain that whatever may be repeated with admiration of the wits of the last generation, or of our own, that on the whole this species of brilliant vulgarity, which made a reputation for a Douglas Jerrold, is rapidly losing ground in cultivated society.

There is a character to be very frequently met with, which is too often imitated by those desirous of acquiring an easy, independent tone in conversation. I refer to both men and women who indulge in "churlish flings and boorish slurs" at the present or the absent in a cool, smiling, easy manner, which they fondly believe passes for polished satire and keen irony. Elderly and imperfectly educated fops, who wish to be thought wits and men of the world, are much given to this style of impertinence. It abounds, however, among all the coarser varieties of people, who think by profuse expenditure and costly dress, to cover defects of intellect and of early associations. They think that an elegant air may be put on as a garment. Nothing is so easy indeed to assume as this ironical and personal vein, which is intended to only slightly annoy, without being carried so far as to give serious grounds for a quarrel. It proclaims unmistakably, imperfect culture or real vulgarity endeavoring to masquerade as elegance, though it is by no means unfrequent among those whose associations should have taught them better.

Avoid at all times in conversation all manner of liberties. "Teasing" is a favorite amusement with many, and is not unfrequently carried, as regards youthful victims, to such an extent as to utterly ruin dispositions which would otherwise have been excellent. It generally leads to irritation and insult. Persons who habitually tease in any manner whatever, directly or indirectly, may be possessed of many excellent qualities, but they are not entitled to true respect; nor is any one, who fails in respect towards others, or in regard for their feelings.

The incurable "tease" who cannot refrain from annoyances, is indeed invariably an individual whose intellect is in some respect deficient or disordered, and who is therefore to be avoided. Such persons are frequently gifted with wit, and, occasionally, with polished (not *refined*) manners, but they are dangerous companions, as their irritating disposition is apt to communicate itself to those whom they are in the habit of attacking.

CHAPTER V.

OF CENSURE AND FAULT FINDING.

HOSE who would excel in conver-
sation should beware of censuring.
There are persons who seldom
talk without blaming some one,
or carping, grumbling and disap-
proving. The faults of others
are as their very breath. They
seem to be forever looking down;
and, to judge them by their own accounts, one might
imagine that they had never, in all their lives, asso-
ciated or met with a decent or reputable human
being.

It is unfortunately true that a very large proportion of social conversation consiists of fault-finding,
or of remarks derogatory to the character of the

absent. Here and there, indeed, we encounter a truly noble nature, which recognizes the vileness of abusive gossip and avoids it. I would have the reader adopt such a character as an ideal to be followed out at all risks, at all times, and under every temptation. Let him resolve every morning that no needless word of censure shall during the day pass his lips; and when he shall have so long adhered to the resolution as to feel quite certain that he has cured himself of the vice, he may indulge in the proud consciousness of being at heart not only a gentleman, but a gentleman who has few peers in the first circles of any land.

There are few persons who do not regard a man or woman who never speaks ill of others as of truly noble character. Such instances of magnanimity are rare, but they never fail to be duly honored. In society their words meet with marked attention, for they are invariably truthful, and the world knows that what they say will be discolored by no malice or uncharitableness. Very elegant and highly accomplished women of the world sometimes accomplish this great triumph over the most insidious fault of our nature, and thereby wonderfully increase their abilities in the art of pleasing.

It is within the power of every young person to make and keep a resolution never to utter a word directly or indirectly uncomplimentary to any one If such young persons should be offered a fortune dependent upon success in this, how earnestly would they guard every utterance! And yet no fortune would ever be of such real benefit to any youth as a heart pure and free from all carping and censure.

Owing to a strange delusion, very few are really aware of their own habit of indulgence in this vice, though they readily remark it in others. I believe, indeed, that the worst offenders would be amazed should they learn the truth. If you have any doubt on the subject, set down thrice a day in a blank book, as nearly as you can recal it, every word which you have said of any one which you would not repeat to his face, or have said of yourself. If you occasionally review the volume you will, in all probability, be induced to reform the habit.

CHAPTER VI.

OF COMPLIMENTS.

THE spirit of a compliment is the expression of something agreeable to another person.

It is therefore absurd to broadly condemn it, since the whole art of pleasing is more or less directly that of complimenting. The most benevolent or generous act to an equal, loses much of its value if utterly devoid of compliment — that delicate homage by which we imply that certain excellencies or merits in another have made upon us a something more than superficial impression.

Women — or men — who are not familiar with

3

the world, or skilled in conversation, invariably express, and perhaps feel, a dislike to compliments.
They are either suspicious and doubt the sincerity
of all praise, or, as is more frequently the case, they
find themselves unable to turn the compliment with
an adroit answer or graceful reply, and are consequently rather vexed than pleased with it. Much
of this comes from an uneasy fear of covert ridicule, of being "quizzed" or held at an advantage.
It is needless to say that such feelings or fears never
annoy a cultivated woman, or any one gifted with
proper self respect.

It is true there are compliments to which objection may justly be raised. Some are coarse, some
clumsy, others trivial, and others worn out; but
they almost invariably correspond to the character
and conversation of those who utter them, and if
we are frequently annoyed, it is generally our fault.

But no compliment should be too severely judged,
unless it be manifestly a downright sarcasm or insult in disguise. The flattest flattery implies at
least on the part of the one uttering it, a desire to
commend himself to favorable consideration, and has
a more creditable ground than scandal, satire and
gossip

I have already intimated that the crowning excellence of conversation, as a mere art, is, not to acquire a reputation for excellency in it, lest through notoriety we lose naturalness. To pay compliments well, especially to young women, one should not have the reputation of being profuse in praise, or, as girls sometimes phrase it, of "having the hat-full ready."

Yet as every expression of congenial appreciation and admiration is really a compliment, it is evident that the art should be cultivated — I dare not say studied — since a studied compliment has been declared to be none at all. Sincere admiration, elegantly or wittily expressed, is acceptable to most people, and is the most effective means of persuasion for a lover. And it need not be directly oral. Expressive and respectful glances — not stares, — adroit commendation of certain qualities in other people which are shared by the one you compliment, all belong to the art. If we carefully study any person's tastes, tendencies, accomplishments and associations, opportunities for sincere and pleasing compliments will occur continually.

Of all compliments the most agreeable are those in which the one paying them seems to be uncon-

scious of so doing, and is at the same time warmly
in earnest. When offered in this manner to a lady
she is doubly gratified, — first with the compliment,
and secondly, with her own penetration at having
detected a real feeling in relation to herself.

Beautiful women are readily convinced by a glance
or by demeanor that their charms are appreciated.
All of them, however, who have any claims to culture, will, when the first tribute is paid, be best
pleased with *appreciative* compliments paid to their
intelligence, accomplishments, "spirit," kindness
of heart, tastes, habits, hopes and associations. A
very beautiful woman who believes that she has excited a deep admiration for some quality *other* than
her beauty — especially if it be one for which the
world gives her little credit — is always gratified.
"I heard that you said a very good thing lately,"
"There is an excellent remark going the rounds
which I hear attributed to you," will be found much
more gratifying to a person who has no established
reputation for wit, than to any other. And as
there are very few persons who *never* say anything
worth repeating, it is an easy matter to pay such
compliments in all sincerity.

There are few persons living who are not more

or less interested in the opinion of others. Men, as a rule, are gratified to know not merely that women have praised them in their absence, but even that they have been favorably spoken of to the dames. If you can inform A that you had conversed with B in reference to him, and that the conversation had been such as to give B a favorable impression of A, or had drawn a compliment from him, you will yourself pay an agreeable compliment by referring to it, especially if your words and manner are aptly managed. If B occupy a high position, A will assuredly never forget the fact. There need be neither impropriety or insincerity in thus promoting kindly feelings between people.

After all said on the subject, it is certain that to an intelligent and cultivated mind there are few women of intelligence entirely devoid of personal attractions; and almost every human being, though he or she may have even relinquished all claim to be beautiful, still clings to the very last to a faith in a certain " expression," which, if *properly appreciated*, must raise the whole personality to admiration. And instances are not unfrequent in which women who were either beautiful, piquant, pleasing or " sympathetic," have heard so little of

the language of admiration, that the first report of
a really genial compliment paid them, thrilled
through the heart like fire. This is sometimes the
case when a sister has attracted all the admiration.
There are again instances in which a lady may have
a good enough opinion of herself, and yet be quite
incapable of appreciating the peculiar or real reason
why she is admired. I could cite the instance of a
lover of art, who had a special admiration for the
singular face of a statue in the Louvre, and who had
the strange fortune to find it almost identically realized as a living fac simile in the features of a young
girl who was by no means accustomed to praise of
her beauty. Very often, peculiar associations like
this will render certain countenances charming to
us, which is the secret, by the way, why ignorant
boys and girls, who are without such associations,
are extremely critical and conventional in their
judgment of personal attractions, while men of wide
experience and knowledge are far more generally
appreciative, and more easily pleased. In short,
where we wish to compliment, the opportunity to do
so with sincerity and credit to ourselves is seldom
wanting, when our tastes are cultivated.

Compliments are frequently uttered as good

natured jokes, not to be taken literally, and yet to be accepted as manifesting at least politeness. Thus in a book on Italy, a gentleman while admiring a picture of Louis XIV surrounded by the ladies of his court, is represented as remarking that "he would gladly have been in that monarch's place at that time." To which the painter of the picture — a Frenchman — replied that "he certainly knew no gentleman who could have filled it with more credit to himself, or more agreeably to the ladies. Such a compliment is a mere trifle, and cannot go beyond a laugh and a gay reply, but, as the world goes, with many men and women it would produce a better impression than the most elaborate wisdom.

Do not forget, however, that in compliments as well as in all that you say, the manner, style, address and tone have, in ordinary conversation, quite as much to do with success, as the *sentiment*. Many people smirk when about to speak; others have an intolerable air of *preamble*, which seems to promise that something remarkable (in the opinion of the speaker) is coming. Some acquire a *manner* of saying everything, which is not agreeable, as it betrays consciousness of intending to produce an effect. In short, there is but one rule, — be *natural*

By carefully observing and noting down some scores of compliments, or of remarks which have made an agreeable impression, and by studying and comparing them, the reader will be able to attain proficiency in classifying these butterflies of the social garden, and he certainly will learn to word his own compliments more aptly. This will be an easy matter, since the proportion of people who will cheerfully supply you with such as have been addressed to themselves, is by no means small.

A compliment is nothing if it is not sincere, and it should no more be confounded with flattery, than pride with vanity.

CHAPTER VII.

OF EGOTISM IN CONVERSATION.

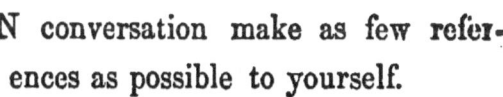N conversation make as few refer-ences as possible to yourself.

Beware of giving the slightest indication that you habitually realize your own merits.

This is, however, equivalent to urging you to begin with first prin-ciples, and to conquer the habit, since no one who has formed it can conceal it.

Egotism is the most insidious and effective poison of merit. No matter how wise, how witty, learned, brave, or beautiful one may be, self-consciousness spoils all its effects, and even a child can render the least vanity ridiculous. It is the greatest of blem-

ishes in social intercourse, and should be most scrupulously shunned in its every form. A French
writer has spoken of people in whose manner could
be detected " suppressed vanity," and of different varieties of such people. The truth is, that the habit
— for it is only a mere habit — must be *cured*, not
disguised. Suppressing egotism does not mean
crushing self-confidence or pride, but the destroying
a silly habit of continually looking at self as another
personage parading about on the stage of life, and
anxiously caring for what is said of it, or studying
the effects which it produces. The fault is rapidly
developed by much indulgence in "small talk," and
above all by continually gossipping of other people
— of families, marriages, engagements, "attentions," fortunes, and what *is said* by everybody of
every body else.

Men and women who are weak and ignorant
enough to believe that a general knowledge of the
affairs of others indicates familiarity with "society"
and the world, are, without exception, egotists of the
ridiculous stamp. Nothing but a weak vanity can
induce man or woman to become the "Jenkins" or
current chronicle of "the fashion" in any city, vil-
lage or hamlet. People not unfrequently encourage

the " Jenkins " by smiles and praise, but they always despise the character in their hearts. It is
very easy to understand that the giving much
thought to little transitory personal trifles of no
value in themselves, rapidly increases the fault of
shallow vanity. He who is continually busy with
reflecting on what people think and say of each
other, will be quite certain to keep a place for himself with the rest. This is the reason why in very
gossiping circles there are few efforts of genius, and
few genial and earnest minds, for all is killed by reflected egotism

Never speak of your own peculiarities.

Many persons acquire a gay habit of merry boast-
ing, or of humorous gasconading — so called from the
Gascons, a brave and talented people, who however utterly destroy all respect for their real merit by their
habits of vaunting. He who would avoid vanity
should have absolutely nothing to do with it — not
even to burlesque it. Self is our most insidious foe,
and he who boasts in fun will soon find earnest
thoughts gliding into the current of his jests. In
short, avoid everything which may suggest, however
remotely, to those with whom you converse, the suspicion that you think of the effect you produce.

There are people who can speak in detail of themselves and their works without vanity, and there are
others who cannot tell you the day of the month
without some ridiculous manifestation of self-
consciousness.

Avoid intimacy with weak minds, or at least
evade as much as possible indulging them in their
idle gossip, if you would escape vanity. Ignorance
takes refuge in personality, and people who care
nothing for books, or art, or amusements, or beautiful
subjects or great questions of general interest *will* talk
about one another and of themselves. "The more
culture the less vanity," is a rule by which one may
accurately determine the nature of the society in
which he finds himself. If you are obliged to associate with back-biters, gossips and egotists, intimate
to them as quietly as you can, and without hurting
their feelings, that you wish to avoid their favorite
topics. If you *persistently* refrain from such subjects for a few weeks you will realize to a remarkable degree the benefit of such discipline.

Persons who can be aware that another is endeavoring to cure himself of a defect, and will yet ridicule him for it, deserve to be distinctly ranked as
morally *vile*.

Taking one vice with another there is not one which makes so much mischief as is caused by censoriousness and gossip, yet we seldom find vigorous efforts made to extirpate them, and it is but fair to inform the inexperienced reader that in circles where there is not a high degree of culture, he will meet with many who regard themselves as very moral persons who will actually discourage his efforts to avoid gossip and vanity. Let him, however, persevere and he will succeed. Life was never given to us that our thoughts should all be given to the betrothals, successes, and private affairs of people, or to what figure we cut before them. Had it been so, there would not have been the slightest occasion for bestowing on us reason or intellect.

Do not in conversation refer *too* frequently to scenes in which you have figured ; to great people whom you have known ; to your travels, your successes, or to anything on which you may be supposed to congratulate yourself. If possible, avoid recurring often to trains of thought and associations connected with your "strong points," since most people, and especially women, are very apt at detecting vanity. Do not however as some do, scrupulously avoid all mention whatever of your experiences and

fortunes. There are men who carry this to an ab
surd degree of affectation, and abstain from the
slightest reference to their travels, or what they
have seen, or of which they were a part. This is
only vanity in a more refined form. Many " honest
folk " expect from a traveller, or any other who has
achieved what is to them at least a celebrity, some
entertaining anecdotes which they themselves may
cite. Such excellent souls can no more comprehend
motives for reserve than an Arab would similar
modesty in a hadji from Mecca. Whenever you
can appropriately and modestly draw upon your experience for an illustration, do so. Rely upon it
that opportunities will not be wanting.

Do not talk so as to display your wealth or your
habitual familiarity with it, or with rich people.
This disgusting form of vanity is very common in
the United States, and gives an excellent standard
for ascertaining the real social position and culture
of many who are well guarded against detection in
other respects. It is an insidious fault, and one full
of temptation in circles where money-getting is the
chief occupation. It displays itself in the affectation of forgetting what some expensive article costs,
and in speaking of expenditures as trifles, when they

were really matters of serious consideration. It is
betrayed in the vulgar habit of never alluding to a
wealthy man without speaking of his riches, or to a
respectable family in moderate circumstances, without declaring that they are "poor as Job." When
you are yourself well off, such a style of reference
to others, especially before those who are not so
prosperous, is truly contemptible, even when no
"hints" are intended, and no offence is given.
This form of vanity is also seen in the habitual endeavor to create the impression that one's mind at
least is familiar with luxury. Such people talk
nothing but gems and divans, Tokay and costly
steeds, sables and three-pile velvet. Others roll
over with a relish, the names of the millionaires of
the day, and will mention with pride the having
been in company, with some great Shylock's agent,
as though there were something gilding in the very
neighborhood of a man who deals in large sums. It
is shown in a tendency to increase figures when
speaking of sums. There are men who, in narrating
an anecdote of a wager never place the sum at less
than "*ten* thousand dollars;" and like them are
the women whose friend's diamonds are always said
to be worth "thirty thousand." The same vanity is

displayed in volunteering to tell the price of every article in your possession, or in asking that of articles belonging to others — a thing which should be done as seldom as *possible*, and always with an apology — or at least with that straight-forwardness which in some persons speaks of itself a pressing reason, devoid of all idle curiosity.

Avoid *very* frequent conversation on any subject in which you are notoriously interested. If you have a specialty in politics, religion, or in any other direction, it will be often enough referred to by others without your introducing it. If you are physically strong, or handsome, or accomplished in any arts, do not make strength and beauty and your favorite abilities, even indirectly, a frequent subject of discussion.

Beware of a peculiar form of vanity which consists in making confidences of your private affairs to many people, and in binding every acquaintance to solemn secrecy as to this or that matter relative to yourself or friends. Weak people often think by such confidence to attract intimacy, but the confided-in seldom fail, on reflection, to attribute it to mere vanity.

Of all foilies, never seek to make capital in gen

eral conversation by communicating to any mortal whatever, your misfortunes, grievances and losses. Whatever momentary sympathy you may attract will, in too many cases, be entirely neutralized on the fatal sober second thought of those in whom you may confide. That is a pitiful vanity indeed, which would sooner expose its defeats from Fortune, than not talk of self. More absurd still is the confession of your private faults and vices — a species of vanity frequent enough among would-be romantic people of a school which is now becoming generally ridiculous. On this subject a French writer has well remarked, that "you should always avoid mention of yourself, since, if it be an eulogium, people will regard it as a lie; while if you criticise yourself, they will take you at your word, and accept it as an article of faith."

In short, never allude in any way, or under any circumstances, where it can be avoided, to your own excellencies or defects.

It is very vain to use strong and emphatic assertions, such as "*I* know," "I am *positively* certain," "Yes — but *I* happen to know *all* about it." It is intolerably conceited, and in most instances irritates, without exciting the slightest respect for

your declaration. Always substitute " I think,'
" I believe," " It seems to me," " Excuse me, but
I think I have heard," &c.' It is not enough to
limit your words in this respect, you should never
emphasize the voice too forcibly. One may say .
' I beg your pardon, Sir," with an expression equivalent to a flat and insulting contradiction.

Still more vain and vulgar is the use of such expressions as " H'm ! " " Pshaw ! " " Much you
know about it ! " " Stuff! " and " Fiddlesticks ! "
These expressions and others like them of a strongly
dissentient nature, should never be uttered by any
one under *any* circumstances whatever. They are
all rude, as is indeed every word and every emphasis which *directly* expresses denial of any assertion.

A very improper manifestation of vanity is shown
in giving advice rather with a view to displaying
superior wisdom, than to really assist a sufferer. A
very common form of such weakness consists in ad-
vising in vague and general terms which are of no
practical significance, and convey no new idea. One
may repeat a hundred times : " be industrious ! be
thrifty ! be enterprizing " — but unless the advice
be accompanied with some practical illustration or
application, its result will in most cases be to irritate

Never talk simply to hear yourself talk, or for effect. Be especially on your guard against this when more than one person is listening to you, for then the temptation will often be great to speak merely from display.

Every time you converse with any one it will be your own fault if you have done nothing to create a favorable impression. But all displays of vanity are unfavorable.

Beware at all times of social oratory. The parlor lecturer is a common form of vanity, especially among men of humble origin who have unexpectedly developed some intellectual power, and risen to a little public consideration. Small orators, small clergymen, small poets and small politicians are all given to this weakness. They love the sound of their own voices and are not in the habit of reflecting that all professional display in private is silly.

Never undertake to *lead* in conversation. Do not when you are about to narrate something look about and enforce silence. If you say good things the world will soon find it out. Never try to be a " lion," or to do all the talking. I have seen a gentleman noted for his stories, look positively offended after having monopolized the entire attention of a large company for an hour, because another person ventured to tell a tale of the same stamp as his own. It is all vanity.

If you remember any one distinctly after a long absence, do not affect to have forgotten him, even though he should be so weak as to do so. Nonchalance is at best an ornament of very doubtful elegance, and is now rather old-fashioned. It is generally accompanied by egotism, and leads every one who deliberately cultivates it into the commission of countless petty falsehoods and many acts of real rudeness. To affect to forget what you really remember is, after all, *untrue* — and honesty is the first qualification of a gentleman or lady. I would lay great stress on the avoiding this affectation of indifference, since it is unfortunately still prevalent in all classes of society. If you really cannot at first recal any one, be certain to speak out honestly (and eagerly, if you feel the *slightest* inclination to do so,) as soon as you begin to remember any circumstance in connection with your former intercourse.

Whenever any instance of vanity or affectation strikes you in others, note it down and strictly avoid it in future in your own person. If you hear a person outshouting an entire congregation in responses or "amens," remember that vanity seeks for effect, and sink your own voice. Nearly all eccentricity whatever is in fact only shallow vanity. Avoid *oddity* of every kind whatever in your external appearance or manners or conversation. If you diligently cultivate your mind and study assiduously to please in conversation, you will soon become noted and that in the most agreeable way.

It is to be regretted that French writers on etiquette and conversation insist so strongly on *vanity* as the real basis of all character. In a work which is in many other respects excellent, I find for instance these axioms:

"It is not necessary to be really modest, but at least attempt to appear so."

"Modesty, or that which seems to be such, is a speculation on the vanity of others." *

Let the young reader rest assured that it is necessary to *be* modest as well as to appear so, and that that virtue *may* be acquired by practice. By associating with those who excel you in your own especial merits, you will improve these, and at the same time

* *L'Art de Causer, Encyclopedié de la Conversation.* Par M. Saint Maurice, Paris 1834.

learn to avoid vanity.   And remember, he who cultivates modesty does not disqualify himself for success in the world.   In acquiring it you also gain confidence and firmness.   Impudence is generally the
cloak of indecision and of cowardice.

CHAPTER VIII.

POLITENESS. ITS BASIS. ITS APPLICATION.

THE basis of all true politeness is kindness.

All politeness should be real, and from the heart. If you constantly strive to reason away your prejudices against people, you will become polite. Most of our dislikes have very little foundation. A large proportion of them spring from idle gossip, from fancied slights, or from trials of our temper which we could very easily forgive, were it really our interest to do so.

But it is always our interest to keep on the best terms with every one who is not really bad or disreputable. To do this one must maintain an unceasing watch over his or her temper, and suffer no opportunity to escape, however trifling, of gratifying others. If kindness of heart be the *first* requisite in politeness, it is quite as true that *assiduity* is not less needed.

Let memory be on the alert to recal anything which may be agreeable or serviceable to those with whom you converse, and keep your eyes and ears open to seize the opportunity for any friendly office, no matter how trifling. *Politeness*, be it remembered, includes " polish, elegance, ease and gracefulness of manner, united with a desire to please others, and a careful attention to their wants and wishes." The first step towards achieving grace is to be quietly confident and feel at ease in any society. If your language be good, your knowledge creditable, your personal appearance devoid of eccentricity and if you have learned to avoid making yourself " conspicuous," there is no reason why you should not be firm and assured, anywhere. Do not vex yourself with thoughts of inferiority, but "be yourself to yourself," and a little familiarity with the world will soon teach you the absurdity of timidity. Ease rapidly brings grace if any effort whatever be made to say and do kindly things in a cheerful and conciliatory way.

Exercise your attention and your thoughts when in company. If you find that bashfulness and embarrassment without cause occasionally afflict you in society, banish them by finding something to do or say *forthwith.* Do not stop to argue with yourself but *act* promptly. Ask for an introduction to any body, and talk of the weather or the walking, or the rooms, or any trifles, till something better suggests itself. The first step in politeness is to make such efforts, and they are a duty. In society you owe them to your host or hostess who does not of course like to see a gloomy or embarrassed guest. And you owe them at all times, in all places, to everybody, as a matter of politeness.

Do not think it a matter of indifference whether you pick up a fan for some humble old dame, eagerly or indifferently. If your mind be active, (*and you can make it so* by frequently thinking of such matters,) it will occur to you that a little attention of the kind with an appearance of prompt, earnest courtesy is *very* gratifying to old people ; and therefore you will probably on such reflection show active service with downright good will. And if, a minute after, you have an opportunity to render the same courtesy to the belle of the ball-room, you will find

4

that you do it all the better for your previous service.

The young of either sex should remember that all
the little attentions, salutations, civilities and graces
of " society " are as strictly due in the home circle
to sisters, brothers, parents and others, as at a party,
and that courtesy, like charity, begins at home.
Boys and girls should be taught never to receive
anything from the hands of a servant without expressing thanks, and all services whatever, from all
persons, should be acknowledged in like manner.

The higher ladies or gentlemen are placed in society, and the more refined their politeness, the more
frequently do they speak courteously to servants and
to all humble people.   French ladies and gentlemen
very generally salute their dependents as they would
their acquaintances, while it has been remarked of
the English in the highest circles, that they never
notice the existence of those who minister to their
wants, and worship the same God with them in the
same family-chapel, any more. than if they were so
many machines.   Of late years this discreditable
rudeness has been a little modified, but it is still
very general.

If it should occur to you that an article which

meets your eye in a newspaper would interest a friend,
do not neglect or forget it, but take measures so that
he may see it as soon as possible. Remember that
to most persons, especially to the young and to ladies, gifts, however trifling, are always acceptable,
and that a shell, a coin, a drawing, in short almost
any little thing is frequently a very gratifying compliment indeed. There may possibly in no one instance be a solid return for all these services. You
may fancy that you are coldly thanked, and that your
courtesy has been churlishly received. But do not,
as the vulgar do, grumble over it, to yourself or to
others. Remember that you have at least exercised
your heart and your manners. Persevere in your
attentions to every one, and you will soon find the
reward *in yourself.* Remember the Arab proverb
" do good and throw it into the sea. If the fishes do
not observe it GOD will."

By remembering all the instances of true politeness, devoid of a desire to *display*, which fall under
your notice, and by applying them, you will soon
become graceful in manner if not in body. The one
however leads to the other. Begin by strictly observing all the little courtesies of thanks, salutations,
offering places, handing chairs, paying deserved com-

pliments, and in fact by rendering all services and attentions to all people at all times, which are proper and fit. Do not neglect anything of the kind, even to a person for whom you care very little, nor say to yourself: " he will never know it if I neglect it." Be up and acting. It is a great step towards politeness, grace and skill in conversation, to have formed habits of generosity and constant courtesy.

If you have an enemy, and an opportunity occurs to benefit him in matters great or small, act like a *gentleman*, and do him good service without hesitation. If you would know what it is to feel noble, and " strong within yourself," do this secretly and keep it secret. Though you have no higher motive, carry out the principle for the sake of pride and dignity. A man who can act thus will soon feel at ease anywhere. It is said of Callot, an eminent French artist and engraver of the seventeenth century, that he was once slandered in a pasquinade by a certain nobleman of the court. At that time, to have one's portrait engraved by Callot was an object of ambition with the highest dignitaries of the kingdom, and it was attained by very few. Callot's answer to the injury was to publish a superbly execut-

ed likeness of his enemy, with an inscription setting
forth his titles and great deeds. To this day the in
cident is cited as an instance of proud nobility of
soul. Callot was in the highest sense polite.

Politeness is shown by passing over the faults and
foibles of those whom you meet. Cultivate this
especially towards relations. The world is severe in
its judgment of those who expose the faults of
kindred, no matter what the provocation may be.
Vulgar families are almost always at feud. It is not
polite to detail injuries which you may have received
from any one, unless there exist some *urgent* necessity for so doing.

Politeness is manifested in courteous inquiries after
the friends and family of those whom you meet, and
in manifesting a cordial interest in them. It is
shown by devoting a little space in every letter to
" remembrances " for friends. It is a highly gratifying form of politeness to write occasionally to all
from whom you have received kindnesses which will
warrant you in so doing. It is polite to conform
your dress, and (in reason) your habits, to the tastes
and feeling of those whose guest or associate you
may be. It is polite and complimentary to inquire
after any one of whose acquaintance your friend may

have reason to be proud. It is polite when you are a guest to endeavor to enjoy yourself and make others do so. It is polite to those who are assembled in any place, to avoid heated argument, and all noisy remarks or "remarkable" conduct. It is polite to promptly ask every one to take a chair who enters your house or office, and the more cultivated you are, the more widely will you extend such courtesies to humble people. It is polite to do everything for another which would gratify him or her and is not unreasonable. It is polite to make no allusions to age. It is polite to spare people elder than yourself, and women of any age, any exertion of personal effort, even in the merest trifles. It is polite to take no notice whatever of accidents or annoying occurrences, unless by so doing you can be of assistance. It is polite to make ready and unstudied sacrifices of your exertion or of your comfort to gratify others; as, for instance, to always escort any lady, or do a service for a friend. It is polite to suppress your peculiar tenets in religion or politics before those who differ with you. It is polite to never take it upon yourself in any way to punish any person, unless it be distinctly your business to do so. It is polite to avoid practical jokes. It is

polite when you have offended any one or hurt his
feelings in any way, to apologize for it, as clearly
as possible without reservation or excuse, since the
more vulgar a man is, the more does he obscure and
degrade an apology by self-justification. It is polite to express an interest in or admiration of that
which is dear to others. It is sometimes more polite
to accept a gift or a courtesy, especially from humble people, than to refuse it; and it is polite to show
the *utmost* kindness and courtesy to those who have
been reduced by adversity. And it is something
more than polite to interpose and shield another person from mortification, wounded self-respect and loss
of dignity.

The young reader may practise the politeness
which will advance him in the most elegant society,
in every hut and workshop. He may show it every
time he speaks to any person, and test it in every
act in which another is concerned. If in addition
to constant courtesy and kindness he cultivate the
graces, be neat in person and attire, make a good
bow, is prompt at offering a lady his arm, and become
otherwise personally dexterous, he will have done
much to qualify himself for that *conversation*,
which, as meaning "familiar discourse and inter-

change of sentiments," must itself be entirely qualified by the nature, habits, and feelings of any one maintaining it.

I trust that if the reader who aims at this accomplishment will carefully re-read this chapter, and *thoroughly* realize the meaning and applicability of its rules, he will not accuse it of being a collection of "mere general remarks" of no practical use. Certain minor requisites popularly connected with " politeness " are indeed not to be learned from a book. To bow gracefully, to hold one's head erect, to sit properly at all times and always at ease, to walk well, to avoid clownish attitudes and many little awkward acts, *to eat properly and conduct one's self well in all respects at table*, require either familiarity with people who do all these things, or else very great perseverance. But to form, even unaided, the great basis of all elegance and politeness, is possible to all. It is a duty and should be a pleasure:

CHAPTER IX.

OF STORIES, ANECDOTES, AND PUNS, IN CONVERSATION

T is well to be able to tell a good story, but it is better to be able to avoid the reputation of being a professed story-teller.

The same is true as regards repeating anecdotes, puns, quotations, and other illustrations of a more formal style of wit or of sentiment than conversation usually affords. He who aims at conversing well, must avoid a hobby.

Yet in limiting your stories to one or two, while in the same party, as high authority advises, I do not counsel the continual repetition of only one or two stories. It is very disagreeable to be expected

4*

to laugh at something which one has heard before, and the man who is known by repeating a small budget of the same tales to all his friends, is invariably more or less imbecile. What shall I say of men who learn *one* story of a professor of elocution, who practise it frequently at home, and repeat it for years on every occasion!

Do not tell a story unless you think it new, or are at least confident that it will be new to your auditors. Let it be *in place* — that is to say, illustrative of something which has occurred in conversation, for a story forced in at all hazards is very ridiculous. Of such awkward introductions the jest books contain the following illustrations:

"An old gentleman had a story of a gun, which he was wont to tell every day at dinner. As it was sometimes difficult to find an opportunity to introduce it, he hit upon the following unfailing expedient. Stamping on the ground beneath the table, he would exclaim:

"'Bless me! what's that?—a gun? By the way, talking of *guns* —'

"And then he told his story."

There is also an instance of one who, in company with a celebrated theologian, thought it necessary to display some Biblical knowledge, but could not, for a long time think of anything which seemed apt. At last, at a very unfit time, he cried out :

" I do declare that Samson was the strongest man that ever lived."

" Not so," exclaimed one present. " You yourself are stronger than Samson."

" How so ? " asked the other, in amazement.

" Why, have you not just lugged him in by the head and shoulders ? "

The jest was rude and therefore not to be commended. In telling stories, study brevity, and good, clear English, avoiding all " fine language," and yet omitting nothing which can render them perfectly intelligible. If you can tell them without laughing yourself, the effect is generally thought to be thereby improved.* The best story-tellers seldom mimic the voice or accent, as it savors of buffoonery and vulgarity, unless a foreigner be described, and even

* CHARLES LAMB, in his *Essays of Elia*, (Edition of Philadelphia, 1859, p. 489,) declares the axiom " that a man must not laugh at his own joke," to be a popular fallacy, and " the severest exaction surely ever invented upon the self-denial of poor human nature." " This is," he continues, " to expect a gentleman to give a treat without partaking of it ; to sit esurient at his own table, and commend the flavour of his venison upon the absurd strength of his never touching it himself."

in such a case, good taste shows itself by avoiding exaggeration.

Never vamp up an old story with new dates and faces. It is a species of falsehood, and will subject you to contempt when detected — as you certainly will be. I have heard one who would be indignant at being called other than a gentleman, tell a story hundreds of years old, as having occurred within his own experience, and to his neighbors. What is to be thought of a man who would risk his character for veracity and honor for the sake of a jest?

An effort at dramatic *acting* in story telling is to be avoided, since it not only leads to "over-acting," but conveys an unpleasant impression of self-consciousness of humor. I do not refer in this to any truly natural effusion of merriment, such as many natives of Continental Europe display in narration, but to the manifest effort at effect which results from vanity.

There are men who are always the heroes of their own stories, and others who will fondly ask: "Did you hear that little thing I got off the other day?" Some will modestly preface a jest by informing you that it is their own, but perhaps you have already heard it, as it is all over the town? Others will incidentally give themselves a touch of gilding by casually mentioning the name of some eminent man or woman who was much delighted with their wit, while certain persons humbly angle for a little praise by inquiring if it be not good enough to *print?*

Many who would not be guilty of an " immoral " thought, do not hesitate to tell *coarse* stories and utter rank jests. As such wit or humor invariably indicates *vulgarity*, either inherent or acquired, I cannot too strongly warn the young reader who would converse well, against even listening to such stuff, lest his mind should acquire a taint. Uncleanliness in any form, unpleasant details of personal neglect, anecdotes founded on the secrets or the articles of the toilette, instances of gross appetite, or indeed of any sensual excesses; of being disgusted, and incidents of ill-health, are all utterly unfit subjects for pleasantry, and should never be used as such. No prefacing or apology can render them excusable, or remove the stain of nastiness from the mind which entertains them. It is worth remarking, that while the merely " witty and wicked " jest generally flits away into forgetfulness, the *coarse* joke remains to be too often permanently fixed in the memory. But young minds which are contaminated with coarseness are the readiest receptacles for all vice. It is not at all unusual to hear, in rural districts, even pious men, of the ruder class, who would not for the world make the faintest allusion to anything savoring of "immorality," still indulge in many varieties of verbal filth which would cause some of the wickedest worldlings of the cities to feel unpleasantly. Those who have carefully studied children's minds, will agree with me when I attribute the development of much of that impropriety which after (and sometimes before) the age of puberty, results in vice; not to inherent appetite, but rather to familiarity with the coarseness disguised as humor, which is never reprobated as wicked, though it may be frequently reproved as "vulgar."

Let the reader rely upon it, there is nothing manly or spirited in any manifestation of coarseness whatever, and that all vulgar wit and humor simply excites the silent contempt of the well-bred man or woman of the world,

Anecdotes should by all means be new; old ones are little insults. A French author has said that we should be very economical in using even the best, as they form a sort of small change, of which a man of wit and taste will avail himself only on very great occasions. A good anecdote, aptly told, is, however, a powerful aid in conversation; serving, it may be, for a very brilliant illustration. A man who never tells an anecdote is generally dull; one who does little else in conversation is frequently described as being in his anec-dotage.

I do not agree with a writer on conversation* who exhorts his readers to invariably attribute the paternity of puns and conundrums to some other person, adding, "if they have a success in the world, you can always reclaim them. But it certainly is not necessary, neither is it in good taste, to begin or end by informing the hearers that such an elaborate effort of wit, as a pun often *seems* to be, is your own. Depend upon it, that if you originate many plays upon words, you will acquire quite as much reputation as a punster as any man need desire, though you conceal your share in them with the most scrupulous care. Genial humor or brilliant wit, far from injuring real dignity in the eyes of cultivated people, increase it; but there is something petty in the continual torture of language for the sake of

* St. Meurice.

extracting forced resemblances, which is generally well understood, and indicates the cause why the professional punster is never spoken of, as such, with much respect.   It has been thought that as people in the olden time *hired* their cap-and-bell punsters, while modern society gets its own for nothing, that they are on the increase; but there is certainly no corresponding increase in the degree of respect which they elicit.

Good puns are, however, not to be despised.   They may point a moral, illustrate a character, and give force and elegance to a compliment.   A pun on the incident of the day may have a vast influence, and pass into history as a curious fact.   When Charles the Fifth boasted that he could put Paris into his glove (alluding to Ghent, or Gand, which was pronounced like *gant*, a glove), he made, it is true, a poor pun, but illustrated, with characteristic force, not only his power, but also the prosperity of Flanders.

It is well to learn from jest-books and other sources, what puns and facetious anecdotes are already current in the world.   If the reader has any aptitude whatever for such matters, he will thus

be soon sufficiently well-informed to be on his guard
against those who would impose on him the shoddy
of wit for its broadcloth. 'Every man," says a
writer, " ought to read the jest-books, that he may
not make himself disagreeable by repeating ' old
Joes ' as the very last good thing."

CHAPTER X.

OF QUESTIONING. ITS MISAPPLICATION, AND ITS ADVANTAGES IN CONVERSATION.

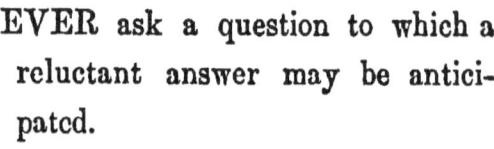EVER ask a question to which a reluctant answer may be anticipated.

I do not here refer to questions put to satisfy prying curiosity, but rather to a form in which some persons shape much of their conversation. The habit is one which incessantly involves those who are questioned, in difficulties. Instead of remarking that the weather is fine, the questioner asks if the weather be not fine? which can be answered only with a commonplace affirmative. Without meaning it, he either puts another in the position of one unable to say anything, or compels an unusual amount of thought and evasion.

The questioner asks at a party, " What do you think of Miss A's dress ? " thereby casting all the responsibility of saying anything unfavorable on the other, or at least safely leading him, or her, into the temptation.   Many show a great, but not credit-able, ingenuity, in employing questions in such a manner as to make others appear to discredit, and yet seem very little in the wrong themselves.   If there be a manifest unwillingness to answer the query, the one putting it will smile significantly, and say : " Oh — I see ; " or, " Ah ! — a friend ? — I beg pardon."   Women of a certain grade of vul-garity seem to think this form of speech very arch, and shrewd, or " cunning," and employ it freely. It is, in fact, a species of " teasing," and is resorted to as giving the querist a position of ease and supe-riority.*

Most of my readers have met, or will meet, per-sons who once or oftener in a conversation inquire, vaguely : " What do you think of A., or B. ? " ex-

---

* MR. CHARLES DICKENS has in the character of " Rosa Dartle," in his novel *David Copperfield,* set forth, with great skill, many of the annoying traits of the habitual questioner in conversation.

pecting no news, but hoping for a display of weakness or dislike on your part. Such persons are tho serpents of society. It is an *art* to evade them, and with them all impertinent, meddling, and foolish questions. The self-possessed conversationalist will, however, find it an easy matter to answer with a calm, steady, prolonged gaze, before entering a polite demurrer against being thus witness-boxed.

Questioning may, however, at times be made a medium of true kindness and courtesy. People are often willing, nay, anxious to communicate information, but· are unable to do so unless adroitly questioned. A modest man, who will not speak of his own exploits, may be induced to impart much that is interesting, and he will frequently, and perhaps very properly, think he has been entertaining others, and conversing in a highly creditable manner.

It is necessary to learn the art of asking questions skilfully, but it should not be forgotten that they ought, in most cases, to be prefaced with an excuse or some slight apology.

CHAPTER XI

TAKING LIBERTIES. IMPUDENCE. STARING.

HOSE whose conversation is inspired by courtesy and refined by culture, are the last to indulge in the violations of etiquette known as taking liberties.

There are circles, and those not entirely among the so-called vulgar, where liberties are continually taken, and where there is even an impression that social intercourse without them would be dull and spiritless. This belief is encouraged by axioms to the effect that "there is nothing like a little impudence to succeed with the women," "nothing venture nothing have," "brass is better than gold," and nothing is given without asking."

The practical meaning of it all is that the modesty of others may be invaded, and the ordinary observances of society freely violated, whenever it suits the pleasure of any one to do so, especially if he can by tact or luck escape punishment.

Let the young reader determine from the beginning that anything which is to be obtained by impudence may be secured to much greater advantage by modesty, or at least by a careful observance of all the forms of good breeding, and by respect. Firmness and confidence, enterprize and boldness itself, have nothing in common with impudence, and the most daring deeds are best accomplished when the most scrupulous regard to the feelings of others which circumstances permit, is observed.

There are men who cannot take a seat in a public vehicle, who cannot give an order at a hotel table, in a word who can do nothing while observed by others, without displaying the miserable vanity of impudence. They ask the simplest questions with the air of "confidence men," and read a newspaper with a pitiable expression of conceit and insolence. They are quick to take offence, for they are aware that they are frequently observed and understood by their superiors in good breeding, even among those whom they treat as inferiors, and the consciousness makes them irritable. To remedy this they take liberties and defy the consequences.

A very common form of vulgar impudence is the staring at ladies. To do so in any public place is ungentlemanly, but to avail oneself of a vicinity which circumstances render unavoidable, is contemptible. The man who will stare continually at a lady across a hotel-table, or in an omnibus, deserves to be arrested. Ignorant young men frequently do this under the impression that it is not really disagreeable to the other sex and that they are in fact paying a species of compliment. Could they know the vexation and annoyance which is often masked under the air of calmness with which their insolence is received, they would think differently. I have heard at a hotel, of instances in which ladies delayed their meals for hours; subjected themselves to many annoyances and even left the house in order to avoid the presence of some conceited puppy who possibly imagined that he was recommending himself to their good graces.

I have known a man who moved " in the first cir-

cles," to intrude into a private opera-box and take a
front seat accidentally left vacant, which he was permitted to retain, since each of the two parties in the
box supposed he was a friend of the other, when in
fact none of them were acquainted with the fellow.
It is difficult to comprehend that the temporary advantage derived from such conduct could counterbalance the permanent contempt excited when the full
nature of his impudence was finally understood by
all.   Yet a liberty of this nature is of the kind
which many persons regard as rather funny and par-
donable.

Never infringe on any properly established regu-
lation be it what it may.   A young lady may be as
dashing a Di Vernon as ever lived, and a girl of the
utmost spirit, originality and independence, without
plucking flowers in public places where it is for-
bidden, or asking questions which she knows will
be reluctantly answered, or intruding where she is
not wanted, and young men may in corresponding
manner behave themselves with all regard to the feelings of other people without incurring the slightest
suspicion of " slowness."

Always discourage forwardness in others and be

reluctant to grant favors or patronage to impudent people. For all *creditable* employments they are less fitted than the well bred and firm, while their honesty is always questionable. Insolence is of itself a lack of conscience as regards the rights of others

CHAPTER XII.

OF ARGUMENT IN CONVERSATION. OF MEN WHO ARE "ALWAYS IN THE RIGHT"

ARNEST argument should be avoided in society or before a third person. To prove yourself in the right is to show that another is in the wrong. It is ill-bred to do this before witnesses, and it is courteous to avoid it, so far as is possible, at any time.

Men are much more given to "argument" than women, and are far less sensible of its absurdity. It is well to reason with oneself as much as possible, but little, beyond a display of vanity, is gained in debating a point with another.

For a man or woman of intellect to seriously ar-

gue a point with one of inferior mind, experience, or culture, is ridiculous.

If you are known to hold firmly established views on any subject, beware of conversing much on it, except with those who perfectly agree with you. You will not aid your cause or yourself by *disputing* over it. If you are boldly attacked, respectable people will give you much more credit for gracefully evading a strife of opinions, than for entering upon it. *Ladies* who have a true claim to the name, invariably appreciate and admire such conduct in a man. Much more skill and sagacity may be shown in refusing to argue, than in so doing; the one who seeks to escape having the great advantage of being able to make his adversary appear determined to be disagreeable and discourteous.

The inconvenience of having a guest given to argument, and one who continually proves himself to be in the right, is well illustrated by a French story which I translate, and which may serve as a lesson for all conceited and disputative men.

" The author of the poem *Des Saisons* — The Seasons — the Marquis de Saint Lambert, introduced one day to the celebrated Madame Geoffrin, who assembled at her house the first men of letters of her time, an estimable man of learning, known by many excellent works which he had written on political economy.

"Madame Geoffrin received him kindly,—as she did every one,— and then the recommendation of the Marquis de Saint Lambert was, with her, of great influence.

"For three months the poet's protegé never failed to be present at the lady's receptions, and no one complained of his company, since he was a man, not only of learning, but of taste. One day, however, when about to enter, a servant stopped him at the door, and said with great gravity :

" ' Madame cannot see you to-day.'

" ' How — she is gone out ? But I see Monsieur Morellet enter — and Monsieur Thomas. Why, there is the Abbé Delille, humming an air at the window. — Ha ! good day, Monsieur l'Abbé ! How is our dear lady to-day ? I'm sure she's at home.'

" ' Madame, sir, cannot see you.'

" ' But is she ill, then ? Of course not, since I hear Diderot's loud laugh, and if Madame Geoffrin were not in health — '

" ' Sir, I beg your pardon a thousand times, but I have simply to say that madame *cannot see you.*'

" This argument was irresistible, and the author bowed to the servant — for a true philosopher is polite to every one -- and went next day to his patron to tell him of the event of yesterday.

" He could make nothing of his strange reception. Had he committed some blunder? Had he permitted himself to say something indiscreet or inconvenient? The author endeavored, but in vain, to show that he had been in the wrong, in order to prove that Madame Geoffrin was in the right. Saint Lambert listened to the end, and only interrupted the eloquent pleading with the words, ' you are in the right, my friend; a thousand times in the right.' When he had concluded, Saint Lambert took from the chimney-piece a letter, of which he broke the seal, and presented it to his protegé, inviting him to read it. The latter urged a few scruples, but finally opened the letter. It was signed by Madame Geoffrin, and, addressed to the Marquis de Saint Lambert, contained the following lines :

" ' I close my door, my dear marquis, on your learned M. B——; should I see him often, I should be vexed to death ; and, thank heaven, I am still a little attached to life, thanks to your friendship and to that of a few of the faithful who resemble you

Your M. B—— is, in short, intolerable — *he is always in the right !* '

" These few words at once explained every thing
to the learned man, and Saint Lambert, as we are
assured, gave him a long lecture on the danger of
being always in the right, and on the necessity of
being sometimes in the wrong. A man who never
risks a mere opinion, who always bases himself on a
logical foundation, on reason, and truth, must be
very annoying.

" The learned author at once changed his system
of tactics, and soon re-entered the good graces of
Madame Geoffrin. M. B—— kept his word. He
became one of the most amusing men of the circle
whence he had been exiled; and his conversation,
bristling with paradoxes and odd caprices of wit and
humor, ensured him many successes. He became
one of the most perfect men of the world of his time,
without in the least losing his reputation as a political economist."

In France the manifestation of a fixed determina-
tion to argue, is very properly regarded as rude.
Even in inferior society we may hear uttered, as a
reproach : " *Tiens ! — il veut avoir du raison !* "
" Ah ! he wishes to prove himself to be in the

right!" Those who have seen a whole dinner-party made uncomfortable by two desperate debaters; or who have heard, in a party, voices loud in dispute, while the hostess, seriously annoyed or grieved, almost struggled with tears at the interruption to the harmony of the meeting; will agree with me that argument in society is indeed misplaced. It is wrong to be always in the right.

CHAPTER XIII.

OF THE INFLUENCE OF WOMEN ON CONVERSATION.   MARRIED LADIES

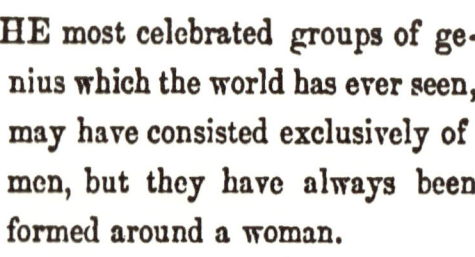 HE most celebrated groups of genius which the world has ever seen, may have consisted exclusively of men, but they have always been formed around a woman.

From the 'days when all the intellect of Greece gathered about Aspasia, down to the French salons of the last century, each with its beautiful or witty *coryphæa*, or centre of the chorus, we find that when conversation has at any period been raised to a high degree of culture, and exerted a decided influence on the spirit of the age, it has owed its development in a great degree to women.

The ability displayed by Dr. Johnson and Oliver Goldsmith in conversation was due to their own ge nius, but their many defects of rudeness, or of eccen- tricity, may be fairly attributed to a want of famil- iarity in early life with women of culture and refine- ment. The best part of Lord Chesterfield's wit and polish, was derived as he himself tells us, from assid- uously frequenting the society of ladies.

Every well educated, amiable and witty woman who has fully acquired " the art of society," has it in her power to exercise, in connection with hospital- ity, a very great influence on the world around her, and to do much good. It is not enough for the scholar, the artist, and others of retired habits to meet with friends among women — they also require intercourse with cultivated society where they may rub off the rust of retirement, and realize with pleas- ure that they are really in the world, and of it. When drawn together around an accomplished hos- tess their thoughts are more readily refined, and the rough diamonds of their knowledge are cut and pol- ished into the most attractive forms.

Such women intuitively comprehend their mis- sion, and recognize that its chief duty is to be agree- able to *all*, and to elicit from each a display of his best qualities. They are consequently courteous and attentive to all who are presented to them. The young collegian or clerk, the retiring youth who has seldom attracted notice from other women, is often astonished and gratified to find himself an object of kind interest to some far-famed belle or brilliant lady-leader of society, whom he had supposed far too elevated by adulation to bestow on him more than ordinary civilities. He does not know that it is her pride to make something graceful out of such raw material as his mind presents, and that the more a woman is elevated by her own abilities, the more widely do her rays shine on all.

It is under the auspices of such women that conversation; the art which of all others conduces to make social intercourse agreeable; is most perfectly developed. The beneficial influence which they exert is in consequence incalculable. The eminent statesman, the great clergyman, the celebrated poet, may imagine that the evenings spent in chatting with an accomplished lady and her friends have been passed in mere amusement, but they are mistaken Genial influences are the most conducive to fresh exertions of genius. Original ideas are more rapidly developed in the summer of cultivated society than in the winter of solitude.

It is a duty which every one owes to himself to seek the society of such women, nor is it less the duty of every lady who is conscious of possessing ability, to exert it so as to assemble these who may be thereby benefitted Let her endeavor by reading, to qualify herself to converse intelligently with every one, and banish from her manner all vanity, and every tendency to say anything disagreeable, so that only pleasant impressions may be left in all. If she do this successfully, she may rest assured that she does not live in vain.

It is to be regretted that in England and in America " the world " seems to think that refined social intercourse can only exist when favored by wealth. To pass an evening pleasantly there must be, for many, a supper, expensive dresses, and the costly preparations which give a festival air to such assemblages. Many women who are personally in every way well qualified to do incalculable good, exclude themselves, in consequence of limited means, from society, and confine their influences to the domestic circle. The result is that ladies when married, and when their minds are expanding in culture and experience, find themselves too frequently shut out from their proper sphere, while mere boys and miss-

es, in certain circles, constitute and control society !
Intellect is transferred from the head to the heels, and
when we ask what is discussed at parties, the appropriate answer would be, " people dance."

This will be remedied, and conversation will become what it should, when the silly spirit of osten-
tation is subdued, and people learn that it is possible to receive friends without turning their homes
into restaurants.   A lady who receives company has
enough to do in attending to her guests, and in promoting conversation among them, without the additional anxiety lest a supper be well served, and lest
servants should blunder.   Our American married ladies complain, and justly, that they lose social influence when they gain the wedding ring, but it is in
their own power to remedy the evil.   Let them receive their friends freely without feeding them.   In
our large cities, receptions without "refreshments,"
or with very little, are already doing much good, but
through the country the old-fashioned ideas of " parties " and what they should be, are still prevalent.

Young men for their part should remember that
excellence in conversation, and refined manners, are
most readily acquired by the " temperate," and that
the man is to be pitied who cannot enjoy social in-

tercourse without eating and drinking. He who
would influence others, must not himself be influ-
enced by appetite. The lowest orders, it is true, cannot imagine a cheerful assembly without the attrac
tions of the table, and this reflection should induce
all who aim at intellectual culture to endeavor to
avoid placing the choicest phases of social life on
such a basis.

It is almost needless to advise young men to cultivate the society of ladies. This counsel is every
where given. But the reader should remember that,
to use a French expression, "there are women and
women," or, that there are very great differences in
"the sex." A young woman who never cultivates
her mind, whose reading is confined to second-rate
novels, whose conversation runs principally on other
people's affairs, and whose remarks have for the most
part a tone of jeering flippancy and depreciation
may be a subject for occasional amusement, but is
utterly unfit to be a friend or companion to any ra-
tional man, and least of all to a man who is steadily
determined to improve in every way his heart and
intellect, and to rise in the world. Fortunately it is
seldom needful to choose between such female friends
or none. He who reads much, who expresses him-

self well, and who talks no scandal, will, if he make every effort, soon find congenial society.

Conversation with intelligent married ladies of any age, who have seen much of the world, is therefore to be strongly commended to all who would improve their minds and manners. To gain a good wife one should study good wives. "He who would the daughter win," says an excellent proverb, "must with the mother first begin." By beginning in social intercourse from above instead of from below, one is far more likely to meet with young ladies who are really worth knowing, than if he devote his leisure hours to idle chat with girls who take no interest in any object of real intellectual value.

CHAPTER XIV.

OF DISAGREEABLE SUBJECTS IN CONVERSATION.

 HE reader will frequently be reminded in society of the remark, attributed I believe to Dr. Samuel Johnson, that "nice persons have frequently nasty ideas." I do not refer to immoral or indecent, but to *disagreeable* subjects, or at least to such as it is well to avoid if possible.

To be scrupulously cleanly in every respect should, with a well bred man, be so much a matter of habit as to seldom occupy his thoughts when not engaged in its duties. But there are people so self conscious of their neatness as to make a constant parade of their customs in this respect. They will talk in any society of the details of their toilette, and descant on the advantages to be derived from cold water as though it were a new invention.   Others are fond of discussing their own ailings, and will describe a dyspepsia or liver-complaint at any time to almost any body.   Some will enter upon such unpleasant personal details with an apology, while others with still greater caution contrive under the guise of an excuse for not fulfilling an engagement, to give the full particulars of the maladies which prevented attendance.

Can it really interest any one to know that a person has an excellent or an indifferent appetite, and does it never occur to others that it is seldom agreeable to a guest to be informed before company that he is eating very little ?   Is it less polite than it would be to exclaim, " why, how much you are eating ! "   When a lady carefully informs all present that she seldom requires much food, does it suggest to those who are even slightly acquainted with physiology, any agreeable associations, and does it prove anything except that she neglects to exercise and to otherwise take proper care of her health ?

We all know that dental operations, the sufferings endured from tight boots, the offensive conduct of

bad servants, children's teethings, the effects of medi-
cines, casualties and deaths, must not only occur, but
also be more or less discussed. But many people
who are by no means absurdly fastidious naturally
avoid all such subjects of annoyance in conversation,
while others, in proportion to the vulgarity of their
minds, introduce them and dwell upon them. There
is of course nothing so easy as to prove the necessity of talking on such matters, but it is very certain that refined people instinctively avoid a griev-
ance, or a personal detail, and experience no inconvenience from so doing.

I trust that the hints given in this chapter will
be borne in mind by the young reader not merely
"in society," but among his most familiar associ
ates. The habit of talking on disagreeable and personal topics is generally formed among intimate companions, and when formed is apt to betray itself at
all times. As with all subjects for reform, it should
be attended to in the root, and not in the branches.

CHAPTER XV

THE PARADOX IN CONVERSATION.

 OMMON -PLACE, steady men, talking among themselves, may be very well amused with "regular stories," perhaps with long ones, and with old-fashioned jokes. But with women, and volatile men of the world, such formal fun finds little favor. Again, an anecdote which would set the table in a roar at the Club, will be but indifferently received at a "reception," even though whispered to dames who are anything but prudes, and though the jest in itself be anything but improper.

"Why is this?" Has the reader never observed that women who enjoy humor such as pleases men invariably resemble men in other respects, as regards habits of thought? Let him therefore think twice before he ventures to offer to ladies the same fun which has already had a brilliant success among his male friends.

Compliments in a witty or droll form are, as I have said, always acceptable to every one. A paradox is also almost invariably sure to at least pass as worth hearing. It is something which, while contrary to received opinion, or *seemingly* absurd, is true in fact, and of a truth which is at once felt by all to whom it is addressed. To say, for instance, of a lady's face in a picture gallery, that it represents either the ugliest of all the beauties, or the most charming of all the plain women, is a paradox which may contain much truth relative to the character of one of those peculiar countenances which attract us; we know not why. It is a paradox to say that nothing lies so much as facts, unless it be figures, since these, while acknowledged to be the most accurate means of presenting truths, are also very extensively used in reports to falsify them. "There is no fool like a wise fool," "Men who are willing to die in the last ditch for their country, are generally careful to avoid the first," are all tolerable paradoxes

Sometimes a paradox occurs in the form of an answer. "Did you ever see such a diamond?" inquired a lady, referring to an enormous imitation-brilliant in a jeweller's window. "Not since I visited a glass-factory," was the reply. "I can read you like a book," said an illiterate person, rudely to a girl. "I should think so," she quietly replied.

The paradox is easily cultivated, and when made on a topic of any importance, is not unfrequently very suggestive of sound reflections. The mind may be trained to form it as readily as the pun; but it has this great advantage over the latter, that it may involve almost any *thought* whatever, while the pun is a mere play upon words and sound.

The paradox is not an element of first class importance in conversation. It should not be very frequently repeated, and it cannot be sustained for any length of time, save in humorous argument. But it should be cultivated as a means of presenting, in a spirited form, thoughts which would otherwise sound very commonplace.

There are those, however, who abuse this form of thought and of expression; as, for instance, men who, having satisfied themselves by much special study and research that some generally received opinion is false, or that some popular idol had his secret faults, frequently, in mixed society, startle and confound people of very ordinary attainments, with their novel views. When the paradox in this form is launched at a person of equal ability, no objection can be raised, save the proviso that there shall be no heated argument, unbecoming general society. But it is unkind and cowardly to unsettle or demolish the perfectly harmless faith or opinions of those who are inadequately provided with powers of repartee.

The urging of paradoxes in this extreme form, especially among those who are not accustomed to them, not unfrequently fails entirely to produce the effect anticipated. I may quote, for example, a gentleman who spent an evening in astonishing a circle of young ladies by abusing General Washington. He flattered himself that he had created a sensation — the only result was a very natural suspicion as to his sanity

CHAPTER XVI.

OF SELFISHNESS IN TRIFLES.　SMALL SACRIFICES.

O MAN can go well through the world, succeed in society, or become an adept in conversation, unless he learn to sacrifice selfishness in many little things to the comfort of others.

It is true that accomplished men of the world are often intensely selfish beings. But they have the shrewd tact to yield in trifles, while some of the most generous people will, through mere inertness and *moral laziness*, never think of giving up or making way, for the convenience of others.

With many women — not *all* — great acts of generosity, and noble deeds are regarded as obvious dutics, while little sacrifices and trivial courtesies have that sweetest of aromas — the incense of voluntary active homage. Hence it comes that men who are known to be cruel, unprincipled, depraved and heartless, are often greatly liked by " very nice" girls — to the great astonishment of male friends who, having exposed the character of "the villain," expect to see him at once detested. These excellent persons do not know that to superficial women, whatever their moral education may have been, great virtues are always a little below the heroic standard in value, while small virtues are very great. It is the old story of the two sexes — the one dealing only in large notes and paying heavy bills, so that he expects every one to recognize the value of money, and the other familiar with nothing but the constant rattle of small change.

But however good and virtuous and great a man may be, he is very far from being excused on that account from making every effort to excel in little virtues, and in those small sacrifices of comfort which are really offered to urbanity. If bad men make themselves attractive, good men should beat them at their own weapons, and there is no reason why they should not. The world is rapidly

losing all its respect for that ungainly and uncouth
Puritanism which in its excess of zeal for grace, lost
all sight of the graces. No degree of moral purity
can afford the slightest excuse for a man's feeding to
gross excess at a table, displaying meanwhile in his
conversation little save conceited boorishness, snub-
bing his hostess at intervals, insulting his fellow
guests in the style of Dr. Johnson and other eminent Englishmen, and finally rolling off to an easy
chair to ruminate at leisure until the hour arrived to
deliver his evening discourse. Yet such is the picture which is drawn of one of the most popular
English preachers of the present day, and it would
apply to many others of less note. Such examples
have the worst possible effect on the young who
are shrewd enough to feel that there is, and should
be, a connection between refinement, courtesy, and
all *true* goodness, and that selfishness and boorishness are as wicked in their ultimate effects on others, as the breaking any precept in the Decalogue.

The man of talent, far from being excused from
cultivating courtesy and small unselfish traits, is the
very one who should lead in such accomplishments.
In the first place, as I have already intimated, all
ability is most perfectly matured and developed by

intercourse with society. And in the second place, the man of great intellectual power is the one of all others who should excel in making himself and those whom he may meet, mutually agreeable. Some of the most brilliant men who ever trod the floor of a parlor, have been " mere scholars," and members of a class which is habitually spoken of among those who are ignorant of its highest types as " pedantic " and ignorant of the world.

One of the most agreeable of small sacrifices which can be made at an evening party, for the sake of the hostess and for the promotion of gayety, is to distribute the conversation. It is doubtless very comfortable to get into a quiet corner with a brilliant beauty, or "a lady-comrade of established liking," and flirt or laugh away with her till supper time. But if one does so, all must — with somebody. Hence the establishment of " barricades " — those settled groups, which cannot be broken up, and which are the horror of all who detest a stiff party. They gather chair by chair till the whole room becomes impenetrable, and any person who is in the charmed circle is to you as " unattainable as the stars." In such a fixed condition appeal to the friend with whom you are conversing, or call your

6

hostess to counsel, and you will soon thaw the frozen stream. No lady who knows much of society will think that weariness of her conversation induces a gentleman who knows his duties to the world, to take leave of her after a prolonged interview, nor will any gentleman suffer his vanity to be piqued should she manifest a willingness to converse with others.

If you have very few acquaintances, make others. This may be readily done by exercising a little tact. It is well to ascertain who are present, from some friend; the doing so will afford an opportunity to intimate that some one of them interests you, in which case courtesy will suggest an introduction. It is needless to say that when it devolves on you to make strangers acquainted, you should exercise some discretion, and ascertain, or at least consider, whether it would be mutually agreeable. Those who introduce much are good Samaritans in society, those who do so injudiciously are marauders who rush upon travelers and bind them captive, two by two.

If you know anything of music, you may properly enough ask for an introduction to any lady who has favored those present with a vocal or instrumental performance. Few singers are sorry to learn that they have made an impression. If there be a man or woman of celebrity, present, it will be but natural for you to desire an acquaintance. If you are in any degree intimate with your entertainer, you would show a kindness which will be appreciated, by intimating a desire to be introduced to any present; especially to any ladies; who seem to be silent and neglected. In the social garden wall-flowers are weeds, but like many weeds they only require a little culture to take place with the choicer blooms.

If you are invited to pass an evening at any place never be one of those who are absent on account of unfavorable weather. Then, if ever, you should make every exertion to fulfil the promise given in your acceptance. A sacrifice of this nature is always appreciated. If your circumstances be moderate, and it should be the occasion of expense which you can ill afford, regard it as a debt of honor which must be paid, and save it out of some other expenditure. Remember that in any case it will not have cost you so much as it will the lady or gentleman to whose kindness you owe the invitation.

CHAPTER XVII.

OF CONVERSATION AT DINNER-PARTIES,

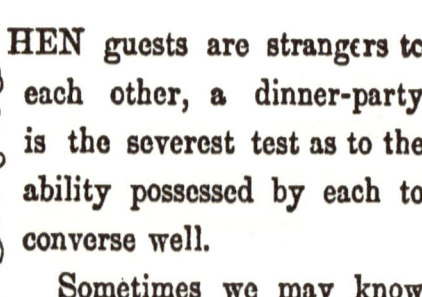

HEN guests are strangers to each other, a dinner-party is the severest test as to the ability possessed by each to converse well.

Sometimes we may know from the character of the host or hostess, or of "the house," that of those who assemble there. It may be "ultra-fashionable," "moderately fashionable," or "rather fashionable." It may be "extremely conservative," "highly respectable, or 'very respectable," and again it may be one of the numerous crosses of two or more of these. It may be based on rising wealth with new affiliations through the younger branches, or by marriage, to the respectable and fashionable, and it may consist of nice, quiet people, forming a sort of unknown island, which maintains very little communication with the great continent of society. It may be diplomatic, or only political, and it may be sectarian. The lady of the house may have been deeply steeped in Parisian French, while her husband is as decidedly immersed in Pennsylvania German. It may be the party of a rising young professional man, or that of one who is firmly established in the world; or of a real estate auctioneer, or prominent editor; or it may be military, or naval, or rural.

If you know thus much of your entertainer, you may probably conjecture something as to the general character of those whom you are invited to meet. Of one thing you may be certain, that the more highly cultivated the guests, and the more decided their cosmopolitanism, the easier will be the intercourse, and the less apparent any want of previous acquaintance among them. There is a freemasonry among men and women of the world which renders a dull dinner impossible. Much tact is often displayed by the entertainer in seating together persons of a congenial disposition, who will readily engage in animated conversation, which acts as a stimulus to all around, and is all the more effective since it ren- ders occasional silence less liable to observation.

If you are seated by a lady who seems reserved, plunge into general subjects and current topics, tak- ing care, however, to make your beginning apropos to some trifle which the dinner itself cannot fail to suggest. On such occasions, general information on small matters will be of great assistance. Lead your neighbor to speak on some subject with which you may happen to be familiar, and as soon as she dis- plays any familiarity with it, encourage her by cour- teous questions to proceed. If she say but little, talk all the more. There is no soil in which some- thing will not grow if it be properly cultivated, and no woman who will not converse in time. If there be a lion of any degree of celebrity whatever, pres- ent, though he be only the local clergyman, you may appropriately enough ask for information relative to him, or bestow it. Much may be done in ascertain- ing where your fellow guest has travelled, and in in- ducing her to speak of the celebrated persons whom she has seen or met. Avoid all egotism whatever, direct or implied. Many persons seem to think that among strangers it is necessary to give auto-bio- graphic hints sufficient to show that they are entitled tc consideration. Rely upon it, if you converse well encugh to excite interest, the world will soon know everything about you.

I have presumed an extreme case, and the most trying-which can happen at a dinner,— to be seated by a diffident woman, or, what is the same thing, by an over-cautious person, who for a long time casts on others the burden of the conversation. Absolute re- serve, from any one, under such circumstances, is unpardonable — it is a lack of courtesy to the enter- tainer, and a reproach to the quality of the guests. With any person who is not reserved you should enjoy conversation. If you are possessed of the slightest general knowledge of men and things, of the current topics of the day, of books, or of places, it will be your own fault if you cannot find some- thing to say, and gradually expand it to animated narrative or discussion. Be always on the alert to *suppress yourself* when you see that your companion is beginning to listen with interest to his own voice ; and when others also begin to listen or to take part in the conversation, be prompt to show them every courtesy and deference.

Never forget that at a dinner, as on all occasions of hospitality, it is your chief duty to relieve the hostess from every annoyance or care.

It would be well if those who give dinners; as well as their guests; would bear in mind the following remarks of a French writer:

"It must not be imagined that the dinner to which you are invited, is simply given for the purpose of giving a gross and purely material pleasure; no, it is to put you in company with persons of consideration, and to give you an opportunity to display your intelligence, or cause your good qualities to be appreciated in the species of demi-intimacy which may result from it."

To which may be added these remarks on dinner parties, and other social meetings, at the present day:

"If you have no accurate ideas as to any of the thousand trifles which rise up at every instant when one has entered a *salon*, observe in silence, and imitate what you see done by well-bred persons. The aristocratic element being that which now prevails at the tables of all respectable families, and in every parlor where good company assembles, it will be easy to do this simply and adroitly, *without aiming at producing an effect.*" *

It has been said that the table is the touch-stone of a gentleman. He who may successfully conceal vulgarity in every other phase of life, is sure to betray it almost immediately at dinner.

* *La Vie Elegante a Paris. Par le* Baron de Mortemari Boisse. Paris, 1858.

CHAPTER XVIII.

OF SILENT PEOPLE. TIMIDITY. ITS CURE.

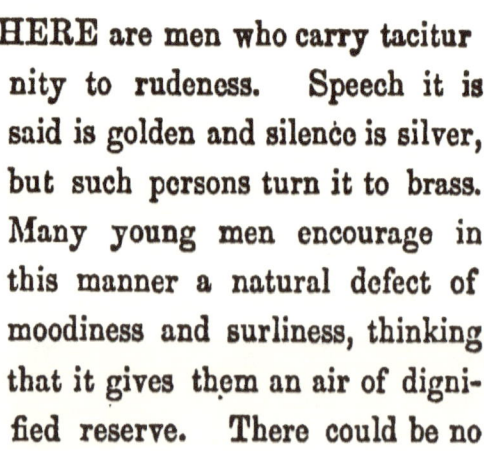

HERE are men who carry taciturnity to rudeness. Speech it is said is golden and silence is silver, but such persons turn it to brass. Many young men encourage in this manner a natural defect of moodiness and surliness, thinking that it gives them an air of dignified reserve. There could be no greater mistake. When a person has given you no positive cause for desiring to drop his acquaintance you are guilty of great rudeness in compelling him to bear the entire burden of conversation. It is an ill-bred assumption of superiority, and of cynical indifference to others, such as can find no place either in the heart or manners of him who would perfectly acquire the humane art of conversation. To endeavor to create an impression of dignity by mere silence is a confession that the outward appearance is not sustained by the intellect. There are however, many persons, and singularly enough the majority of them are women, who are silent in society and avail themselves of every art to create the impression that their silence is the result of courteous attention, when in fact they have nothing to say. Among weak and shallow persons of their own calibre their tongues will fly rapidly enough, but with strangers and especially with all who are out of their own "set" they are afflicted with a most disagreeable dumbness, varied by little "flurries" of mere shallow "talk." It is remarkable that people of this kind when they eventually find their tongues, are extremely apt to employ them in sustaining differences of opinion and "arguments," which leave on the whole an unpleasant impression. With such persons an accomplished conversationalist may at least practice patience and display good temper. He will often make a highly favorable impression on them, and be afterward astonished to learn it, when no word at the time indicated his success. Should he persistently return to the charge he cannot fail to achieve a complete victory.

There are occasional instances of young persons of excellent dispositions and even of high intellectual culture, who are afflicted with reserve and bashfulness to such a degree that it actually becomes a species of mental disease. Parents say of this that " it will wear off," and frequently leave it to cure itself. It may indeed outwardly pass away, or be transformed to an affectation of assurance or of impudence, but its evil effects are too generally felt even to the end of life, in the want of that calm confidence and well balanced presence of mind, so requisite in all intercourse with our fellow beings. In such cases a study of the art of conversation, with efforts to put into practice its rules in company with a few intimate friends, will be found amply sufficient to effect a cure.

He alone can become a *truly* accomplished conversationalist who is gifted with a kind heart, and such a person will always take pleasure in conquering the painful diffidence of others, and in breaking away the limits which separate them from " life."

Many persons suffer most unjustly under the im-
putation of having nothing to say, when the truth
is, that few comparative strangers have ever conversed much with them.   I believe it will be found
that, in most cases, these "silent women" and
"dumb youths" are far better worth knowing than
the majority of chatterers of common-place trifles.

If you are so unfortunate as to feel a tremor at
the thought of encountering strangers in society, remember that they simply form a collection of persons, with whom you would have no difficulty in
conversing singly.   If you are conscious of possessing general information equal to that of those whom
you expect to meet, and are yourself respectable
as regards personal appearance, venture confidently
and calmly on the ordeal.   You will soon find it
is like learning to swim, and that there is no difficulty or danger, even in the first plunge, which is
not entirely imaginary.   Let nothing deter you,
come what may.   If in certain circles you meet with
people who are unkind enough to be indifferent, or
annoy you more directly, take no notice of it ; above
all, do nothing to revenge yourself, and console your
mind with the indubitable truth, that if you avoid

acting as they have done, the time will come when you will be far their superior as regards the practice of all in "the art of society" which can make you truly esteemed.

Every evening spent in society is a lesson which, if turned to advantage, may aid your success in life.

CHAPTER XIX.

OF CORRECT LANGUAGE IN CONVERSATION.

O SPEAK your own language correctly, is to secure the most important aid to success in society.

Study the grammar and dictionary carefully and continually, but avoid unusual words and high-flown phrases.

If you have a well-educated friend, ask him, in confidence, to observe and correct your faults of language. If your own education has been defective, and your opportunities for mingling with cultivated persons, limited, you will probably use many expressions which, you will be surprised to learn, are, if not incorrect, at least to be avoided. Do not suppose them

to be trifles. In good society, the slightest inaccu-
racy in language will be greatly to your disadvan-
tage. No advantages of person or of fortune, can
entirely counterbalance the effect of a phrase, or
of a peculiarity in pronunciation which betrays
early ignorance. But if you converse *correctly*,
you certainly possess an accomplishment which will
enable you to sustain a position in any society.
When it is once acquired, you need experience no
timidity in talking with any person whatever —
your language will of itself entitle you to a courteous reception. The number of persons whose expressions are entirely free from mistakes, or impro-
prieties, is so small, that one belonging to it is sure
of respect.

You would do well to form a class with a few
friends, for the purpose of reading aloud by turns
some well written works. Select a chapter, and determine, by the aid of your dictionary, the proper
pronunciation and accent of every word. In the beginning, read the separate chapters over at least six
times, or oftener, if you are not confident of having
perfectly mastered every difficulty which each presents. If there be added to this, practice in writing
short " compositions " or essays, to be submitted to

the criticism and correction of the whole class, your progress will be rapid.

It is very difficult to make young persons of either sex comprehend the positive impropriety of using slang. Its words and phrases are, for the most part, expressive, and occasionally humorous. When we experience difficulty in expressing a thought concisely and with point, a new application of some cant word not unfrequently settles it very promptly. And this latter is indeed the great impediment with which those who would converse correctly, expressively, and fluently, have to contend. A slang phrase is really "a lift for the lazy," which saves trouble in thinking. But for this very reason it should be avoided. Endeavor to exert your ingenuity in forming some correct equivalent for the slang expression. Determine what your thought is, and express it in good grammatical language. Remember that those who converse with the greatest purity, and at the same time most impressively, never employ slang.

The young man who converses readily in simple and correct language, possesses an accomplishment which cannot fail to aid him materially in the pursuit of fortune or of honors. The first indication of genius in Henry Clay which led to his advancement, was his constant endeavor, while yet a mere boy, to express himself with purity and accuracy. Such a habit is generally received by the world as indicative of *strength* of character, while slang, bad grammar, and provincial phrases, are often thought to betray the weakness of self-contented vulgarity.

Ladies frequently use slang phrases, with a slight pause or smile to serve as marks of quotation, or rather as an apology. But to modify a fault is not to remove it. Resolve that you will never use an incorrect, an inelegant, or a vulgar phrase or word, in any society whatever. If you are gifted with wit, you will soon find that it is easy to give it far better point and force in pure English, than through any other medium, and that brilliant thoughts make the deepest impression when well worded. However great it may be, the labor is never lost which earns for you the reputation of one who habitually uses the language of a gentleman, or of a lady.

It is difficult for those who have not frequent opportunities for conversation with well educated people, to avoid using expressions which are not current in society, although they may be of common occurrence in books. As they are often learned from novels, it will be well for the reader to remember that even in the best of such works, dialogues are seldom sustained in a tone which would not appear affected in ordinary life. This fault in conversation is the most difficult of all to amend, and it is unfortunately the one to which those who strive to express themselves correctly, are peculiarly liable. Its effect is bad, for though it is not like slang, vulgar in itself, it betrays an effort to conceal vulgarity. It may generally be remedied by avoiding any word or phrase which you may suspect yourself of using for the purpose of creating an effect. Whenever you imagine that the employment of any mere *word* or sentence will convey the impression that you are well informed, substitute for it some simple expression.

If you are not positively certain as to the pronunciation of a word, never use it. If the temptation be great, resist it; for rely upon it, if there be in your mind the slightest doubt on the subject, you will certainly make a mistake.

Never use a foreign word when its meaning can be given in English, and remember that it is both rude and silly to say anything to any person who possibly may not understand it. But never attempt, under any circumstances whatever, to utter a foreign word, unless you have learned to pronounce correctly the language to which it belongs. If you have not been able to acquire the tongue, remember that "French without a Master," or any similar work, will enable any one, with a few hours of careful study, to pronounce at least tolerably.

Many young men are so ignorant as to believe that the theatre is not only a school for elegant manners, but also for language, and that expressions picked from "genteel comedy" may be properly used in ordinary conversation. I regret that it is *not* entirely needless to say, that this is a very vulgar error. Neither in England nor in America does the stage at the present day present anything much better than a gross caricature of good society and of its manners. I would not forbid the theatre, by any means, as a place of amusement, any more than I would a Punch and Judy show; but after many years of familiarity with the drama, as set forth by its best artists, I can say conscientiously that I regard the youth as one to be pitied who derives from it his lessons of life or language. However correctly an actor may pronounce English, he seldom fails to fall into a strained and exaggerated style of emphasis and of action, which, if introduced into daily life, would be simply ridiculous. His business is to intensify all that is extravagant in life, while the province of good breeding is to subdue it.

Do not, however, aim at acquiring a great reputation, or rather notoriety, for using elegant language. Should you do so, you would probably endeavor to sustain it for the sake of display, and could not fail to become affected. The great charm of conversation is to be natural, and this is unavoidably lost to every one who is *conscious* of exhibiting in a superior manner the medium through which he expresses his thoughts. Remember that when according to Whately, we exclaim of an orator: "how eloquent!" the true eloquence no longer exists.

SELF EDUCATION,

CHAPTER XX.

OF ACQUIRING GENERAL KNOWLEDGE.

 NE may converse well at times without displaying knowledge, but still a certain amount of learning is essential to all who would excel in conversation.

The literary information which enables one to maintain a creditable position in social intercourse, is two-fold : — that which results from a regular education, and that which is derived from the casual reading of current literature or through occasional study.

It is possible for almost every one whose education has been neglected, to repair the loss to such a degree that it will be unnoticed. To do this, a regular plan and steady application are all that is requisite. Knowledge increases knowledge very rapidly He who every day adds to his stock, and also reviews

7

something already learned, will find in time that he knows more than he has read, for he will have awakened observation and thought.

THE STUDY OF GEOGRAPHY.

I will suppose that the reader who is desirous of becoming well informed, has at least mastered the most ordinary branches of a common school education. Let him, then, review his geography with scrupulous care. Ignorance of the situation of countries and their cities is unpardonable, and such blunders in conversation are ridiculous. I have heard a University man, who spoke four or five languages, ask if Sumatra were not in America. In connection with the careful study of geography, one should gather from books of travel, and from history, and from reviews, all the latest information relative to each country.

I have already spoken of the advantage to be derived from the association together, in a club, of persons for improvement in reading. If such a club were also to take up geography, discussing a separate nation at a meeting, each communicating all that he had read or heard on the subject, there would be little danger of gross ignorance of it. As soon as one nation or country shall have been well discussed, its name should be legibly written on a large sheet, and with it a few leading facts illustrating its population, language, history, and government, in the style of the short articles in a gazetteer, which should hang up in the place of meeting till it may be presumed that all are familiar with them. (A very extensive knowledge of the world may be easily gathered, by adhering to the simple rule, whenever you learn anything in reference to a subject, review what knowledge you already have in reference to it.

THE STUDY OF GRAMMAR.

The grammar of your native language, as I have already intimated, should be carefully studied. A good, *full-sized* dictionary should be in your possession — the best that money can buy — though to obtain it you should be obliged to sell every book you own except your grammar and your Bible. Refer to it continually. Let no day pass without determining from it the meaning and proper pronunciation of words with which you are not familiar. But beware, lest, as many do, you suffer the diction-ary to take the place of *memory.*

Bear in mind in studying the grammar, that your object is not simply to commit rules by heart, and to parse, but to converse and write correctly.

If you can associate with you, in studying the grammar, one or more friends, it is not impossible that your progress in learning will be much greater than if you were directed by an indifferent teacher.

After becoming somewhat familiar with the general principles of the language, it will be time to begin to read aloud from authors noted for their purity of style. For this purpose, I recommend Goldsmith's "Vicar of Wakefield," Washington Irving's writings, "The Spectator," and Macaulay's "Essays," and "History of England." Observe, while reading, the agreement of the precepts of your grammar with the sentences which you follow. Remember, that by devoting regular hours to study, and by *frequently* reviewing and understanding thoroughly every page, before you undertake a single new paragraph, you must inevitably succeed.

Having done this for a short time, you may begin to write according to the rules laid down in the ensuing chapter. Your study of grammar will now begin in earnest, and you cannot fail to realize, day by day, its great practical utility.

CHAPTER XXI.

OF SELF-INSTRUCTION IN LITERARY COMPOSITION, OR WRITING.

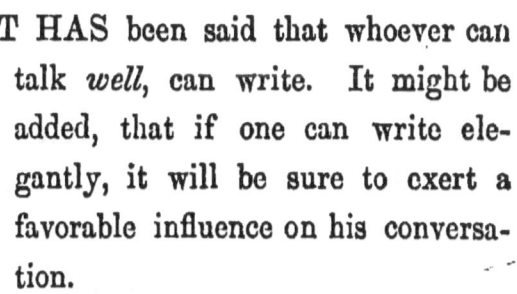

T HAS been said that whoever can talk *well*, can write. It might be added, that if one can write elegantly, it will be sure to exert a favorable influence on his conversation.

If a young man has had absolutely no practice whatever in committing his thoughts to paper, he would do well to obtain some simple and well written work and *copy* from it until the general forms of expression become familiar to him. Letters are excellent subjects for such practice. Having done this till he has filled a few quires, let him form a few reflections of as natural a character as though he were telling something to a friend, and note them on a slate. From these he should write a letter; and, what is of greater importance, should then *re-*write it, with the utmost care, at least once. I have observed that unpractised letter-writers are always perfectly satisfied with the first effort.

Epistolary writing is an art which rapidly culti-vates the mind. It is said that during the Revolu-tionary war, men who were at its beginning very ignorant of composition, yet who were raised to offi-ces which obliged them to correspond extensively, became excellent writers. It has the advantage of being the easiest road to ready expression.

By writing on a great variety of subjects, and by the occasional introduction of humor into composi-tion, the student will rapidly improve in the manage-ment of language, and his letters will be received and read with pleasure. It will be found well worth the while to enter into a book, from time to time, subjects to introduce into correspondence.

When confident that you can write a good letter, correctly, (and not before,) you may begin to com-mit your thoughts to paper in the form of "compo-sitions." Do not begin by selecting "Love," or ' Ambition," as a subject. Rather describe, as ac curately as possible, scenes which you have witnessed, and events which have come under your observation. Let your language be plain and simple, such as you would like to hear from a friend in conversation, and endeavor to use short words. " Fine writing," as it is called, is rapidly going out of fashion, and " sensational " efforts are peculiar to the vulgar. So far as it is possible, write as you should talk, and talk as you would write.

Read aloud what you have written. Many defects will then be perceived which had before escaped your observation. If you have a literary friend who will kindly correct your efforts, submit without argument to his revision; and be certain that in asking him for *advice* you do not, like most young writers, merely mean admiration. Rely upon it that it will be long enough before you deserve the latter. If you can, after months of constant labor, avoid errors in writing, you may congratulate yourself on having advanced rapidly.

Literary composition is of all arts the one best adapted to bring our thoughts and our knowledge into a useful form, and to improve our language. Yet most persons have a great dislike to spending time in steady labor over it, and especially to carefully correcting with the grammar and dictionary what they have written. Many of those who have made a crude beginning, which has possibly been admired by a few friends, must needs "rush into print," and editors are in consequence seriously annoyed by entreaties for encouragement from those whose manuscripts would not bear the revision of any̅ governess who is qualified for her calling.

I would however encourage every one to cultivate the art of writing so far as to be able to " pen an article for the press " when there is an occasion to do so. Such opportunities continually present themselves in America, and may frequently be turned to advantage. Every young man may expect to be on a committee where his services as secretary will entitle him to esteem. No one knows but that the time may come when he will be glad to be able to prepare a petition, a report, or a series of resolutions.

The student should by all means obtain some elementary work teaching the principles of English composition, and study it carefully. It is better to do this, however, after he shall have made some progress in mere copying and corresponding, lest he be embarrassed at the same time by the labor of writing, and of forming his thoughts. Parker's Exercises is to be commended for this purpose, but if it is not to be procured, any schoolmaster or bookseller will doubtless aid the student to obtain some other work on the same subject. The Elements of Rhetoric, by Professor Henry Coppée, (Philadelphia, E. H. Butler & Co.,) and The Scholar's Companion, by R. W. Baily, will at this stage be found to be excellent and most useful works. Whately's Elements of Rhetoric, and Blair's Lectures on Rhetoric and Belles Lettres may next be studied to very great advantage. Those who would go further in this study, and who have facilities for obtaining books, will derive great advantage from perusing the Essays on the Nature and Principles of Taste by the Rev. Archibald Alison, Burke's Philosophical Enquiry into the Origin of our Ideas on the Sublime and Beautiful, Campbell's Philosophy of Rhetoric, and the Elements of Criticism, by Lord Kames.

I can not too earnestly insist on a steady adherence, in writing, to the principle of observing regular hours for study, and of assiduously reviewing everything learned from the beginning. To keep up these reviews *with the least possible labor* is of itself an art, though far from being one which is difficult of application. Geography, which must al- ways be kept up as a study, should, for instance, be frequently made to furnish subjects for literary com- position.. As the student advances in the separate department of the study of literature, he will find that geography embraces, or leads to, the read- ing of books of travel, of history, and of science. Thus the two become at every step more identified. In pursuing literary composition, he will find that all three studies continually present material which is common to each, and that, in consequence, the acquisition of knowledge becomes easier as it pro- gresses.

The student need be under no apprehension that confusion will result from this growing affinity be- tween the different branches of study. Let him perfectly master the first principles as here laid down, continually acquiring fresh facility in their management and application, and he will see his way more clearly as he advances. He will however be materially aided in this by observing the practice of forming groups of facts, and of constantly adding to them, of which I have spoken more fully in another place. Every man, during the course of his life, acquires, and rapidly loses, a vast amount of information which he would retain, were he in the habit of referring each item, as it comes to his knowledge, to some group of facts which he has formed and frequently reviewed.

It is wonderful how rapidly the mind gathers knowledge, and with what tenacity it is retained, after steadily persevering for some months in this practice of noting down certain facts, of adding to them at intervals, and of carefully *learning* the whole by occasional reviewing. Its results in strengthening the memory are incredible, especially with the young.

CHAPTER XXII.

OF READING.

F IT be within your means, obtain a good Cyclopædia. That of Appleton is at present, on the whole, the cheapest and best in English, and it is to be recommended as containing information relative to America which is to be found in no other work. When, in the course of your conversation, or reading, a subject is introduced of which you are not well informed, consult the Cyclopædia as a guide to further knowledge, and as far as is possible, impress the facts on your memory.

The student will derive great advantage from keeping common-place books. Let them be stoutly

bound blank books, with a wide margin. On referring to any subject, enter its name and definition in
your book; adding to it, from time to time, notes of
the additional information which may be acquired on
it. I have found volumes of ordinary sized letter
paper the most convenient for this purpose. Write
down the name of every work which you read, with
extracts from its pages. An author has said that to
read without writing, is to be guilty of downright
folly

Make out a list of the best authors in the English
language in both prose and poetry, giving the prefer-
ence to those of long established reputation, and
read them carefully as opportunities may occur to
do so. Read aloud, at times, from all of them, as
it will assist you materially in understanding each
author's style.

It will be well in many cases if the student begin
by reading essays, biographies, standard books of
travel, and other works of light literature; since
I am convinced that this is the surest means of
acquiring a taste for reading, and of awakening a
desire to become familiar with more solid literature.
Young men desirous of cultivating their minds, often
begin by reading works which, owing to a want of

general knowledge, they find intolerably heavy. I
have frequently known one ignorant of very common
facts, and of well known books, to devote himself
to months of reading of first class historians.   For
want of a few associations of interest, everything
thus read is apt to vanish from the memory almost
as soon as perused.   For this reason I would recommend a careful perusal of many works which are
not generally regarded as " educational; " as, for
instance, Bulwer's " Last Days of Pompeii," which
has been correctly described as the best introduction
to Roman Antiquities.   Let the reader always bear
it in mind that every fact acquired should be either
made the centre around which to group further
information on the same subject, or else be added to
some group already formed, and set down either in
the memory or the common-place book.   If this habit
of collecting and *classifying* knowledge be for a
short time vigorously pursued and rigorously adhered to, the results will be both remarkable and
gratifying.   Every newspaper will be found to contain paragraphs worth clipping out and preserving.
   If a club or society be formed with a view to cultivating knowledge, it will be well for its members
to obtain a few works for reference.   Among these

the following may find place : Lippincott's " Gen eral Gazetteer," Brande's " Dictionary of Science, Literature, and Art," The American Census Report, Chamber's " Cyclopædia of English Literature," and Allibone's " Critical Dictionary of English Literature and British and American Authors." Useful manuals of general literature in the form of catalogues have been published by the Appletons and G. P. Putnam, of New York. To these may be added Mills's " Literature and Literary men of Great Britain," D'Israeli's " Curiosities of Literature," Cleveland's " Compendium of English Literature," and Hallam's " Introduction to the Literature of Europe in the 15th, 16th and 17th Centuries." " Lectures on English Literature, from Chaucer to Tennyson," by Henry Reed, of Philadelphia, is also to be commended, as also the " Handbook of General Literature," by Mrs. Botta.

Every American should make himself thoroughly conversant with the literature of his own country. Let this be borne in mind, and its object pursued with eagerness. There is no more infallible means of awakening and sustaining national pride and patriotism than a knowledge of the genius of your native land, and its results. Shakespeare is half the glory of England. Make it a matter of conscience to be able to recal the name of every American writer of any eminence, and to have something more than a superficial knowledge of his writings. In these days, everything which contributes to create a national feeling is of very great substantial value, and you can materially aid it by teaching yourself and others what we have contributed, as a country, to the history of intellectual culture. If this work should have impressed nothing more than this fact on your mind, it will not have been written in vain.

The reader will find in Dr. Griswold's "Prose Writers of America," and in "The Poets and Poetry of America," (*latest edition*) information which will enable him to make a good beginning on the subject of which it treats. Trübner's "Bibliographical Guide to American Literature," published in London, presents, in the form of a catalogue, the titles of all American works printed previous to the year 1859. It is extremely useful, since it gives, under separate headings, the titles of books published on different subjects, and also contains, in the form of an introduction, an excellent and concise history of American literature.

The study of general literature may be advanta-
geously pursued in the following manner. Let the
student obtain, for example, "The Poets and Poetry
of Europe; with Introductions and Biographical
Notices," by Henry W. Longfellow. Beginning
with what is written of the literature of each language, he should not merely master it by frequent
perusal, but, so far as he is able, follow it up by obtaining and reading the works referred to in the
volume. He will at least thereby make beginnings,
or groups, to which all the subsequent information
on the subject which is met with, may be attached.
He will find something relating to these groups in
almost every good literary magazine, and very frequently indeed in newspapers. Let it all be collected. Copy and clip assiduously. Bring into your
reading circle all facts thus acquired, and discuss
them freely.

In connection with this study, the reader will derive great advantage from carefully perusing, as he
advances, the "Historical Views of the Literature
of the South of Europe," by J. C. L. Simonde de
Sismondi, (Bohn's Standard Library — to be obtained through most booksellers); "The Prose Writers of Germany," by Frederic H. Hedge, (Phila-

delphia, 1848); "History of Spanish Literature,' by George Ticknor; Hallam's "Introduction to the Literature of Europe," (Boston, Sheldon & 'Co. 1863); Max Müller's "German Classics from the XIV. to the XIX. Century," (London, 1858); "Sketches of the Poetical Literature of the Past Half Century," by D. M. Moir, (Edinburgh, 1851); " The History of English Poetry," by Thomas Warton, (London, 1840) ; "The Poets and Poetry of the Ancient Greeks," by Abraham Mills, (Boston, 1854) ; " Specimens of Foreign Standard Literature," edited by George Ripley, (Boston, 1838-9), and " Specimens of the Greek and Roman Classic Poets," translated into English verse by Charles Abraham Elton, (Philadelphia : F· Bell, 1854.) A very extensive series of the works of the English poets has been issued by Little & Brown, of Boston, and many useful selections may be made from the publications of Henry G. Bohn, in London. These books ; a catalogue of which may be obtained from every bookseller ; comprise several hundred volumes of excellent works of general literature, which are for sale in our principal American cities, at a very moderate price. For a knowledge of the shorter current poems of the English language, the student may consult the "Household Book of Poetry," collected and edited by Charles A. Dana, (New York 1858.)

This list might be greatly extended, but the reader may rest assured that long before he can have *carefully* read so many of these works as he will probably be able to buy, hire, or borrow, no difficulty will be experienced in continuing the course of literary study for himself. As he progresses, and his interest is awakened, he may take up standard works of history, and peruse them with real relish. From history he will derive intellectual strength, and its study should be continued through life. As an easily mastered and purely elementary work, the excellent "Landmarks of History," by Miss Yonge, (3 volumes, Philadelphia, F. Leypoldt, 1864), may be commended to young readers.

Let the student avoid second-class novels, and, indeed, a very large proportion of the light works constantly poured forth from the press. To peruse them not only wastes time, but, what is worse, weakens the mind. If it be convenient, one may properly know what is being published, and acquire a general knowledge of its character, without injury, but the greater part of your reading should be devoted to books of established reputation.   It is melancholy to think of the amount of trash over which many men and many more women, debase their intellects.

Never let your reading betray you into pedantry. Its main object should be to make your conversation not only sensible, but also agreeable and *varied.*

CHAPTER XXIII.

MORAL AND MENTAL PHILOSOPHY.

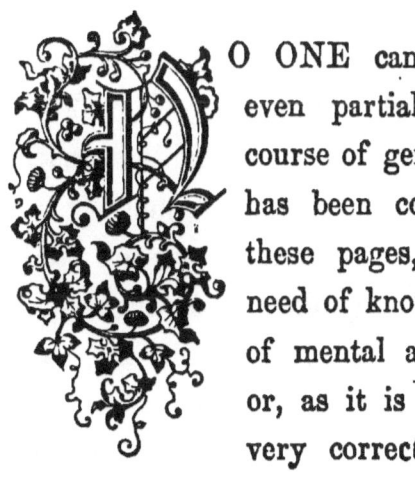 O ONE can have made himself even partially familiar with the course of general literature which has been commended to him in these pages, without feeling the need of knowledge on the subject of mental and moral philosophy, or, as it is generally, though not very correctly termed, of metaphysics.

Erudition is most rapidly acquired by learning as much as is possible of every subject at a time, or in making a thorough beginning, by reviewing our knowledge, and by adding to it. To make a good beginning in general literature, "The

History of Philosophy," by Dr. C. S. Henry, (New York, Harper Brothers,) may be commended, to be followed by the "Biographical History of Philosophy," by G. H. Lewes, (New York, Appleton, 1859,) and Tennemann's "Manual of the History of Philosophy," translated by Rev. Arthur Johnson, (Oxford, 1832.) With these may be consulted "Fleming's Vocabulary of Philosophy," containing a valuable list of writers on the subject of which it treats, edited by Rev. C. P. Krauth, (Philadelphia, Smith & English, 1860,) and "Schwegler's History of Philosophy," (New York, Appleton & Co.) From these works the student will readily find his way to the original sources of which they treat. I commend a careful study of this branch of learning, since it is unquestionably true that those whose minds readily incline to it, find the least difficulty in acquiring and classifying general knowledge. A man who has mastered all the principal formulas and methods of thought which history presents, has acquired the *stems*, so to speak, of all literature, science, and art.

CHAPTER XXIV

OF ART IN CONVERSATION. ÆSTHETICS.

 S ART in some form is fre-
quently made a subject of con-
versation in all circles, it is ad-
visable that every one should
possess some sound information
regarding it.

After a certain progress has
been made in literature, a knowledge of art becomes indispensa-
ble, to enlighten much of our reading. If this be
deliberately undertaken on fixed principles, a few
weeks of systematic reading will be of more real avail
than years spent in irregular "dilettantism," or
looking at pictures and other works by mere chance.

There are very few persons indeed who are en

gaged in manufactures or mechanical occupations of
any kind, to whom the historical knowledge alone of
art would not prove of very great profit.

The study of art in all its branches may be ad-
vantageously pursued, first, in books devoted to its
general history and principles, and secondly, in
detail, as opportunities for study and observation
present themselves. I at any rate advise the reader
who would be a proficient in conversation, to learn
at least the names and characteristics of the principal
pal painters, and their schools; to become familiar
(from engravings) with the different orders and styles
of architecture, and the principal buildings of the
world, and to know something of sculpture. Architecture is very intimately connected with history,
and is, of all branches of study, the one most easily
mastered so far as the general details are concerned.

Let the reader remember that every period of history produced its peculiar language, philosophy or
religion, literature, songs, style of painting, sculp
ture, dress, manners and customs, music, and general tastes. These were all allied to each other, and
grew out of one common national feeling. All of
them were most characteristically reflected in their
architecture. As soon as a new style of architecture

spread over Europe, it was promptly modified by each nation into a sub-style, in accordance with its other arts and habits. If you learn what these different stages of art were, you will have advanced into " the study of æsthetics,'' or " the theory and philosophy of taste, the science of the beautiful, or that which treats of the principles of the *belles lettres* and fine arts."

Do not undertake to talk of pictures or of any works of art whatever, until you have acquired, from reading the history of the subject, some accurate ideas. Unless you do so, you will chatter nonsense, despite all that is said of there being no disputing on " mere matters of taste." There is no such thing as a " mere matter of taste."

A beginning may be made in the study of art from the works of Mrs. Anna Jameson, especially in her " Memoirs of the Early Italian Painters," (Boston, Ticknor & Fields, 1859,) " Memoirs and Essays on Art, Literature, and Social Morals," (1846,) and " Sacred and Legendary Art," (1857.) Also, for general reference, the " Anecdotes of Painters, Engravers, Sculptors, Architects, and Curiosities of Art," by Shearjashub Spooner, (New York, 1853,) and a " Handbook of Literature and the Fine Arts,'

8

compiled by George Ripley and Bayard Taylor,
(New York, 1852,) which are the most easily acces-
sible American works of the kind. For reading, I
would recommend "Lanzi's History of Painting,"
translated by Thomas Roscoe, (London, H. G. Bohn,
1847,) Vasari's "Lives of the Painters," Kugler's
"Handbook of the History of Painting," "The
Philosophy of the Beautiful," by Victor Cousin,
(New York, 1854,) "Ten Centuries of Art," by
H. Noel Humphries, (1852,) "Lectures on An-
cient Art," by Raoul Rochette, (London, 1854,)
"Artist Life," by H. T. Tuckerman, (New York,
1847,) "Works of Art and Artists in England,"
by G. F. Waagen, "Lectures on Painting, by the
Royal Academicians," (London, H. G. Bohn, 1848,)
C. O. Müller's "Ancient Art," "Materials for a
History of Oil Painting," by Charles L. Eastlake,
Schlegel's Æsthetic works, (Bohn's Library, Lon-
don, 1847,) "Art Hints," — also "Art Studies,"
by James Jackson Jarves, (New York, 1862,) "The
History of the Art of Painting," and "Sculpture
and the Plastic Art," (Boston, J. P. Jewett, 1850,)
Dunlap's "History of the Arts of Design in the
United States, (New York, 1834,) and, if accessi-
ble, D'Agincourt's "History of Art, (6 vols., Paris,

1823,) and "Reflections on the Painting and Sculpture of the Greeks, &c.," by Winkelmann.

I do not advise the reader to touch the works of Ruskin until he shall, by previous study of good authors, have formed settled and correct views of Art. In Ruskin there is much real information subjected to the treatment of the rhapsodic, chaotic mind of a man who was, as he boasts, totally ignorant of all that had been written on the subject of Æsthetics by its greatest masters, the Germans. His reputation is principally derived from "fine writing" and bold dogmatism.

I by no means enjoin this course of reading as indispensable. It is simply given that those who have the ambition to qualify themselves for very accomplished conversationalists by acquiring a wide range of general knowledge, may know what books may be safely read. For ordinary purposes, to simply "pass well" when such subjects are introduced, a very few of these books will suffice. Whatever is read at all, should, however, be read very *thoroughly*.

Let the reader beware of finding fault with works of art, unless he is *very* positive from previous study that he is quite in the right. Those who are ignorant of drawing and coloring, are generally the most arrogant in their criticisms. Having " been to Europe " is no proof of a *knowledge* of art, unless it has been accompanied by careful study, and a man who has never seen a great picture, but who has read much, and studied some *good* engravings of great works, will indubitably know far more on the subject than an idle person who has run through all the great galleries abroad.

Beware, too, of indiscriminate admiration. This country is prolific in self-taught, very ignorant artists, whose works are lauded in the newspapers as being equal to anything ever produced by the old masters. Become a scholar, and they will not dazzle you.

Never imagine that any one is " a judge of pictures," or an authority in art, unless you know that he has carefully read its history, and is also a person of literary attainments, or of much general knowledge. If his " taste " has been acquired simply by looking at paintings, he may indeed have picked up many details, and possess " a picture-dealer's knowledge of art," but little else. Painting is so nearly allied to poetry and history, that an ignorant man who has become familiar with the works of the great masters, is a painful incongruity.

When he is, however, a collector, and the owner of a gallery, we may be reminded of the blind man of the Spanish proverb, whose beautiful wife was adorned for the admiration of his friends.

Avoid the frequently repeated and vulgar error, that the old masters were inferior to the modern, and remember that it is only very ignorant persons who sneer indiscriminately at all " old pictures.'' A few centuries ago, most of the genius of Europe, instead of being given, as at present, in a great measure, to practically useful pursuits, was devoted to art; and it is absurd to assume that such efforts, by the world's most intelligent races, did not produce great results. The great lesson of history, and the basis of all true criticism, is to fully understand that every age, and all that it brought forth, form essentially a *whole* with other eras; — that the past was the basis of the present, — and that it is as unreasonable to underrate it by comparison with the present, as it would be to decide on the relative merits of the blossom and the fruit.

CHAPTER XXV

OF STUDYING LANGUAGES.

 O LEARN a language is to prac-tice an art; to study the general principles of languages in their affinities and history, known as philology; is to investigate a sci-ence. In his excellent " Lectures on Language," Professor Max Müller claims that Philology has been raised to the rank of an exact science, with a physical basis.

I commend a careful reading of these Lectures to all who would study language thoroughly In con-nection with them, the reader will derive great ad-vantage from " An Outline of the Elements of the English Language," by Prof. N. G Clark, (New

York, Charles Scribner,) "Modern Philosophy," by Benjamin D. Dwight, (New York, A. S. Barnes, 1859,) "Marsh's Lectures," and "The Philosophy of Life and the Philosophy of Language," by Frederic von Schlegel. Should he find the study congenial to his tastes, he may, after mastering these works, venture to attack the great "Comparative Grammar" of Bopp, translated by Lieut. Eastwick. With these he can hardly fail to guide himself through the different branches of this fascinating science, of which it may be truly said that few tend so much to cultivate and enlarge the mind in its pursuit of knowledge.

I would advise the reader to master his own language so that he may not merely be able to read Chaucer, Gower, Lydgate, and other old English and Scottish poets with ease, — in doing which he can derive much aid from Chaucer's "Legende of Goode Women," edited with a valuable introduction and notes, by Hiram Corson, (Philadelphia, F. Leypoldt,) — but also to obtain something more than a merely superficial knowledge of Anglo-Saxon, which may be done from the "Grammar" and "Analecta Anglo-Saxonica" of Louis Klipstein, (New York, G. P. Putnam.) To learn Greek with its dialects, and even Latin, as our collegians are expected to do, before acquiring the slightest knowledge of our own noble language in its earlier forms, is one of the absurdities which will at a future day seem inexplicable to a more thorough generation of scholars. With the works of Klipstein may be also studied "The Hand Books of Anglo-Saxon Orthography; of Anglo-Saxon Root-Words; and of Anglo-Saxon Derivations." (New York, 1854.)

To study French, Spanish, Italian and German, and Latin, an easy beginning may be made with Monteith's "Languages Without a Master," which work may be had in separate numbers of any bookseller at a very moderate price. Having mastered, let us say, "French Without a Master," the student would do well to procure from the Bible Society in New York, or of any of its agencies, a French New Testament. This excellent institution not only provides the New Testament in many modern languages, with the English version on a parallel column, but is also; according to my experience; extremely courteous and obliging, through its agents, in obtaining for scholars, and others, such translations which are sold at very low prices.

Having read the Testament with careful and frequent reference to the grammar, the student may translate some easy work, with the aid of a dictionary. The Testament will have supplied so many words and expressions, that it will be found a matter of no difficulty. He should then write exercises, which he may do to advantage from " Ollendorff's Method," a very thorough work.

For the student of French who is thus far advanced, I commend the excellent " New Guide to Modern Conversation in French and English, by Whitcomb and Bellenger," Philadelphia, (F. Leypoldt, 1863, " *Trois Soirées Litteraires à l' Hôtel d'Avranches*," (an admirable book) by Mme. C. R. Corson; and for reading, Lamé Fleury's " *Histoire de France*," and " *Trois Mois sous la Neige*," by Jacques Porchat, a work crowned by the French Academy, (Philadelphia, F. Leypoldt. New York, Carleton.) ˊ

The same system may be pursued with the other languages. German may, however, be more readily acquired by substituting for the " Ollendorff" (which, as arranged for this language is very difficult,) a work of the same character, according to the method of Ahn, by Füllborn, (Philadelphia, J. B. Lippincott.)

8*

Let none be afraid lest the study of languages prove too difficult. Let him rather dread his own indolence. It should never be forgotten that every step in learning is easier than the one preceding, and that to a man or woman who has any *real* claim to be intelligent, and to deserve a rank above the incurably ignorant and incapable, I have not advised in these pages a single object of study, or a single book, which can not be acquired or understood by means of steady reading and occasional reviewing.

Having made an advance in French and Spanish, or Italian, (and not till then, since it is best to take the easiest step first,) the student should attempt to acquire a knowledge of the Latin classics in the original, beginning with Cæsar's "Commentaries," and "Cornelius Nepos." For this purpose, I suggest the aid of literal translations. Very great scholars have commended this method, and it was generally pursued when the study of classic literature was at its height in Europe. As has been well said, literal translations direct the student immediately to the order in which words are to be taken, and at the same time at once supply him with their meaning. Experience teaches that words thus learned are more readily remembered than in any other way. The grammar should however be carefully studied, and, if it be possible, " exercises " in the language should be frequently written. In studying Latin, a Latin Bible is invaluable.

I have, since writing the above, met with an assertion to the effect that no one ever learned a language well without a master; and that, with very rare exceptions, no progress of any real value in such studies is ever made, except in the countries where the languages are spoken. The author can within his experience point out a score of instances of persons of not more than average intelligence, who have, without instruction, mastered one or more languages to such an extent, that only a short residence in the respective countries would have given them perfect fluency in conversation. Let it be remembered, however, that *perfection* in a foreign language is rarely attained, and that one has opened the gate to a vast amount of information when he can simply *read* another tongue.

CHAPTER XXVI.

OF CURIOUS AND MISCELLANEOUS KNOWLEDGE.

 HERE are certain little topics of no *great* value, on which it is, however, agreeable to be well informed, since the opportunities for imparting information on them very frequently occur in society, and they furnish innumerable illustrations for " small talk."

When discussing jewelry with a lady, you may entertain her with a few trifles drawn from " The History and Poetry of Finger Rings," by Charles T. Edwards, (New York, 1855,) or from that very agreeable book " *Lithiaka ;* or Gems and Jewels, their History, Geography, Chemistry, and Ana," by Madame de Barréra, (New

York, Harpers, 1859,) or from "Jewelry and Precious Stones," (Philadelphia, J. Pennington, 1856.) At the table, remarks on old China or Sévres may be reinforced from Joseph Maryatt's "Collections Towards a History of Pottery and Porcelain," from "Pallissy, the Potter," or from "The Curiosities of Glass Making," by Apsley Pallatt, (London, 1849.) Sewing may suggest something from "The Handbook of Needlework, from the Earliest Ages," by the Countess of Wilton, (London, 1840,) or Miss Lambert's "Church Needlework," (London, 1854.) Perfumes may be studied in the interesting "Art of Perfumery," by G. W. Septimus Piesse, (Philadelphia, 1856,) or in his "Odors of Flowers," or in "Perfumery," by Campbell Morfit, (Philadelphia, 1853.) At dinners, Doran's "Table Traits, with Something on Them," Brillat Savarin's "Physiology of Taste," Simmond's "Curiosities of Food," and Sayer's "Pantropheon," will suggest many amusing anecdotes of food, and even confectionery affords a number of curious facts, which may be gleaned from the books of Gunter and of Parkinson. Pettigrew's "Medical Superstitions," and Cordy Jeafferson's "Book about Doctors," may amuse when remedies are discussed. "Redding on Wines" contains information for a convivial friend, and the "Anecdotes of Animals," (London, 1861,) is useful for an occasional appropriate story. "Arthur on Family Names," and Lower's "Dictionary of Family Names," are excellent works when that very common subject is discussed; while Bishop's "History of American Manufactures" may be almost daily quoted, and, what is more, studied to real advantage. Fairholdt's "History of Tobacco" contains much that is interesting to smokers. Among other works which will be found useful, are "Hogarth's History of Music," "Musical Sketches," by Elise Polko, translated by Fanny Fuller, and "Mendelshon's Letters," translated by Lady Wallace, (Philadelphia, F. Leypoldt,) "The Percy Anecdotes," "Parlor Charades and Proverbs," by S. Annie Frost, (Philadelphia, J. B. Lippincott,) — an amusing work for social entertainment, — "The Floral Lexicon," "Salad for the Solitary," "Costume in England," by F. W. Fairholt, (1846,) Hone's "Year Book," "New Curiosities of Literature," by George Soane, "The Pocket Lacon," "A Lift for the Lazy," (New York, 1849,) Bohn's "Handbook of Proverbs," "The Rose; its History, Poetry, &c.," by S. B. Parsons, (New York, 1847,) "Flowers for the

Parlor and Garden," by E. S. Rand, (Boston, J. E. Tilton & Co., 1863,) " Opportunities for Industry," (Philadelphia, 1859,) a work containing much curious and valuable information on a great variety of topics, "The Sea," (*La Mer*) by Michelet, (New York, Carleton,) Hoyle's "Games," and " The Book of Chess Literature," by D. W. Fiske. (New York, Carleton.)

Let the reader remember that I by no means urge the reading of any of these works as absolutely essential to culture, bnt as simply supplying some of that agreeable general information, without which mere erudition is apt to appear heavy, if not repulsive, when advanced in ordinary society.

CHAPTER XXVII.

OF SCIENCE.

HAVE, in the preceding chapters, traced the studies of geography, grammar, literary composition, and general literature from their first principles, and shown the reader how it is possible to pursue them to their higher developments, where they may be said, in a certain sense, to blend into one.

I have not as yet, however, spoken of acquiring the practical knowledge that leads to Science, which is far more accurate and searching than the pursuits of literature and of art. In fact, I do not recommend any to follow these studies to their higher branches, even under the influence of a knowledge

of moral and mental philosophy, unless they be
qualified by some acquaintance with science. The
merely. literary and artistic mind is not adapted to
the present age, and its habits of thought lack pre-
ciseness and strength.

The area of scientific study is however so vast
that it is with reluctance I venture to indicate the
possibility of mastering even its principles without
the aid of others. The reader who has acquired
some acquaintance with history, possesses, I will assume, the power to comprehend a general history of
science, from Bacon to Comte. If he has mastered
to any considerable degree the works which I have
indicated in the chapters " Of Acquiring General
Knowledge," and of " Moral and Mental Philosophy," he will readily appreciate the outlines of the
great growth of practical and positive philosophy.
If, for instance, while studying geography, he should
have read the " Comparative Physical and Historical
Geography " of Arnold Guyot, (Boston, Gould &
Lincoln,) or " The Earth and Man," by the same
author, he can not have failed to acquire some
knowledge of the advance of science. A simple and
popular work, such as " Knowledge is Power," by
Charles Knight, Well's " Familiar Science," (Phila-

delphia, G. W. Childs,) or Whewell's "Influence of the History of Science upon Intellectual Education," will now be found useful in preparing the mind for perusing the history of science, and especially those biographies of the great physical philosophers in which it is most accurately written.

NATURAL PHILOSOPHY.

Algebra, and Geometry, and Plane and Spherical Trigonometry should be studied by all who find on careful examination, that elementary works on these subjects present no invincible difficulties. From this point the general knowledge of science becomes, in a great measure, possible or impossible, according to the power of application possessed by the student. The "Primary Lessons in Natural Philosophy," by J. L. Comstock, the "Introduction to Natural Philosophy," by D. Olmstead, Draper's "Text Book," and "Gray's Elements," are works generally used in schools, and being easy to obtain, may be commended as forming a good introduction to practical science. Bouvier's "Familiar Astronomy," (Philadelphia, G. W. Childs,) has been commended by the most competent authority in England and America, as an excellent introduction to the science of which it treats.

For the study of general mechanics, the "Elements of Mechanics," by W. H. C. Bartlett, Boucharlat's "Elementary Treatise on Mechanics," and Renwick's "Mechanics," will furnish a beginning not beyond the grasp of a practical mind, even without a teacher. It is needless to say, that to every intelligent person pursuing this study with avidity, opportunities for improvement are to be found in all mills and factories. In connection with this subject, I would earnestly impress upon the mind of the reader the advice, that he never allow the opportunity of examining any mechanism, or other practical application of science to the useful arts, to escape his notice, and if it be possible, never to relinquish the object till he shall have fully mastered its details. The opportunities for deriving profit from such knowledge occur so frequently in life, that no man ever acquired it without finding it a capital capable of returning a large per centage.

It would be impossible, within the limits of a single volume, to give the details of every department of science, and to commend the best elementary works on each subject. I am the more unwilling to attempt this since every year now witnesses such great advances in this department of human knowledge while book after book is cast like a fresh wave on the beach of learning. I can however assure the reader, that if he has for some months *thoroughly* followed out the plan of self-education which I have thus far laid down, with such assistance as most town-libraries can afford, and if he continues at every step to review what he has already learned, he can hardly fail, after mastering one or more elementary books on natural science (aided by such experiments as his own natural ingenuity may suggest,) to ascertain by inquiry, what works may be obtained on the special subdivisions of mechanics or mechanism.

GEOLOGY.

Among primary works on Geology are the "Elements," (with an Introduction to Mineralogy,) by John L. Comstock, "Elements of Geology," by Gray and Adams, "Elementary Geology," by E. Hitchcock, Loomis's "Elements of Geology," Mather's "Elements," Prof. J. D. Dana's "Manual of Geology," (New York, T. Bliss & Co., 1863,) Trimmer's "Practical Geology," St. John's "Elements," and the "Outlines of Mineralogy, Geology, and Mineral Analysis," by T. Thompson, and the "Geology" by Sanborn Tenney — an excellent work for private students. To these may be added Sir Charles Lyell's "Antiquity of man from Geological Evidences," (Philadelphia, G. W. Childs.) One or the other of these can hardly fail to be within the reach of the reader, and will serve as an introduction to the study in its higher branches. And while on this subject, I would specially advise every one who has hitherto devoted no attention to geology, to resolve that some acquaintance with its general outline shall by all means enter into his scheme of general knowledge. Geology is to Science, what architecture may be assumed to be in æsthetics, or in art; a practical basis for associating the facts of other branches of science, and a record of the history of creation, as architecture is the history of mankind.

CHEMISTRY.

Notwithstanding the rapid advances constantly being made in chemistry, the following works may still be commended as useful for the beginner in that science. Stöckhardt's "Principles of Chemistry,' translated by C. H. Pierce, (Philadelphia, E. H. Butler,) Silliman's "First Principles of Chemistry," Regnault's "Elements of Chemistry," Foster's "First Principles of Chemistry," Gardner's "Medical Chemistry," Murphy's "Review of Chemistry for Students," Porter's "First Book of Chemistry," Lehmann's "Manual of Chemical Physiology," translated by J. C. Morris, and the "Class Book of Chemistry and Chemical Atlas," by E. L. Youmanns. To these may be added for the more advanced student, Lehmann's "Physiological Chemistry," translated by George E. Day, Booth's "Encyclopædia of Chemistry," the "General Notions of Chemistry," by Pelouze and Frémy, and Will's "Outlines of Chemical Analysis."

Chemistry is the most practical of sciences, and cannot, therefore, be pursued beyond a certain point without the aid of experiments. Fortunately, there is perhaps no city in the United States where access to such experiments may not be obtained by every one who is sincerely desirous of knowledge. It is one of the most fascinating of studies, and, perhaps, the most useful of all, so far as its technology, or application to the wants of life is concerned — there being few trades in which some skill in it is not directly profitable. If, in the comparative table of positive knowledge, geology may be said to correspond to architecture, chemistry may, from its infinitely ductile and delicate nature, be compared to painting.

NATURAL HISTORY

The study of Natural History can hardly be regarded as optional to any one who aims at being well informed, since without some general knowledge of animal nature, even geography can be only imperfectly learned. Fortunately, it is extremely entertaining, and presents the great advantage of affording an easy introduction to several other branches of science. Among the books to be used are the "Introduction to the Study of Natural History," by Louis Agassiz, Roschenberger's "Natural History," Smellie's "Philosophy of Natural History," and the "American Natural History," by John D. Godman. For collateral reading, much useful information may be drawn from the volumes of the "Boston Journal of Natural History," the "Journal of the Academy of Natural Sciences of Philadelphia," and from the "Annals of the Lyceum of Natural History of New York." The "Stray Leaves from the Book of Nature," and John D. Godman's "Rambles of a Naturalist," are incidentally worth reading.

BOTANY.

The utility of a knowledge of Botany is so generally recognized, that it forms a branch of study in
nearly all colleges, and schools of a high class.
Those who live in the country, and yet are ignorant
of it, may be said to be half-blind, since they see
nothing of the real life or nature of the vegetable
world around them.   Among the many works on the
subject in general use, are Mrs. Lincoln's "Familiar
Letters on Botany," Comstock's "Introduction to
the Study of Botany," "The Plant," and "The
Principles of Botany as illustrated in the Crypto-
gamia," by H. Coultas, (Philadelphia, 1853 and
1855,) Gray's "Botanical Text Book," (a work
of special merit,) Gray's "First Lessons in Botany," Gray's "Manual of the Botany of the Northern United States," Hovey's "Fruits of America,"
Torrey and Gray's "Flora of North America," —
"the most extensive local Flora ever undertaken,"
— Wood's "Class Book of Botany," Torrey's
"Compendium," Darby's "Botany of the Southern States," and Downing's "Fruits and Fruit
Trees of America."

PHYSIOLOGY.

It has been said by more than one advocate of physical culture, that to know the structure of our own bodies is as essential as any branch of education or learning whatever. It is very certain that there is positively no subject so frequently discussed, on which so much ignorance is displayed, as this. The success of quacks is owing, in a great measure, to the general want of knowledge of the conditions on which health is based; and it is very certain that if the many invalid women, and badly digesting, overworked men of America knew themselves physically, better than they do, we should soon see an improvement in the health of the nation.

"The Physiology" of Dr. John Dalton is unquestionably the best work of the kind as yet written. For elementary study, the reader may take Comstock's "Outlines of Physiology," Corning's "Class Book of Physiology," or Cutter's "First Book of Anatomy." Among other works published in this country, are Lambert's "Human Anatomy, Physiology, and Hygiene," and C. A. Lee's "Human Physiology," J. W. Draper's "Human Physiolgy, and that of Robley Dunglison — a work of decided merit. Magendie's "Human Physiology,' translated by J. Revere, Lowget's "Treatise on Physiology," translated by F. G. Smith, S. G. Morton's "Illustrated System of Human Anatomy,'' Reese's "Analysis of Physiology," Séquard's "Experimental Researches," Carpenter's "Principles of Human Physiology, (Philadelphia, 1853,) Smith's "Anatomical Atlas," Steele's "Elements of General Pathology," Tracy's "Mother and her Off-spring," and, finally, Velpeau's "Elements of Operative Surgery," translated by P. S. Townsend. If this, and several other works which I have mentioned, should be regarded as beyond the reach of most readers without instruction, I can only urge what I believe to be true, that those who have carefully read any elementary and introductory works of physiology, may at least gather much valuable information from all that I have mentioned, even where entire proficiency is impossible.

JURISPRUDENCE.

I recommend every one who is resolved to become truly well-informed, to acquire some knowledge of the general principles of English Law, upon which our own is founded. With this intention, the reader would do well to peruse very carefully "Blackstone's Commentaries;" to become familiar with legal forms as laid down in Graydon, and to at least look over, with some attention, the work on the practice of law which may be most applicable to his own state, the name of which work may be obtained from any lawyer of his acquaintance. Should he desire to go further, he may read "Kent's Commentaries on American Law," "Story on the Law of Contracts," or Parsons on the same subject, and Smith's "Elements of the Laws." All of the works of Geo. T. Curtis, whether on copyright, conveyancing, the Constitution of the United States, or Patent Laws, or on American jurisprudence, are of a kind as well adapted to the use of the general reader, as to that of the professional student, — a merit due to their clearness of conception and admirable expression. I would say, in this connection, that a more general knowledge of industrial jurisprudence, or of laws relating to patents and copyrights, might very well be disseminated in this country, among the many people who are practically interested in such matters.

The works on Medical Jurisprudence by Beck, by Wharton and Stillé, and by Dean, as well as Wharton's "Treatise on the Criminal Law of the United States," with Butler and Heard's "Leading Cases," should be read by every man who may expect to serve at any time on a jury. Having tested the value of such knowledge, I would beg the reader to pay attention to this remark. We continually read in the newspapers of sentences or acquittals, especially in lower courts, and before ignorant magistrates or juries, which could never have been awarded had those concerned possessed simply that amount of merely common-sensible information which any person of ordinary intelligence is capable of extracting from a perusal of the books above mentioned.

APPENDIX

CHAPTER XXVIII.

OF VULGARISMS IN CONVERSATION.

ARE should be taken to avoid in writing, as in conversation, all American, as well as English, vulgarisms. These may be ascertained by reference either to Webster's or Worcester's Dictionaries, to Bartlett's "Dictionary of Americanisms," to "Live and Learn," &c., a work "containing examples of one thousand mistakes of frequent occurrence in speaking, writing, and pronunciation," (New York, Garrett & Co., 1856,) or to the article on "American'sms" in "Appleton's Cyclopædia."

Among the words or expressions to be strictly avoided, are the following, for which I am principally indebted to the works above mentioned:

Advantage, (to) used as a verb, instead of profit.
About right, instead of well, or correct.
Action, instead of proceeding, or decision.
Antiquarian, instead of antiquary.
According to Gunter, instead of accurately dcne.
Accountability, instead of accountableness.
Above my bent, instead of out of my power.
Acknowledge the corn, (to) instead of to admit the charge.
Across lots, instead of in the quickest manner.
Aggravate, (to) instead of to irritate, or to insult.
All-fired, instead of enormous.
All sorts of, instead of excellent, or expert.
All to pieces — smash, Entirely destroyed.
Allot upon, (to) instead of to intend.
Allow, (to) instead of to declare, or assert.
Along. To get along, instead of to get on.
Among the missing, (to be) instead of absent.
Among, instead of between.
Aint, instead of is not.
Anything else. A vulgar affirmative.

Any how you can fix it.

Approbate. A word obsolete in England.

Ary, instead of ever a.

As good, instead of as well.

As well, instead of also. I was angry *as well* as he.

At, instead of by, or in. We should say, sales *by* auction, not *at* auction; and *in* the North, not *at* the North.

At that. And poor at that, instead of also, or as well.

Avails, instead of profits, or proceeds; as, the avails of their own industry.

Awful, instead of ugly, difficult, or very.

Axe, instead of ask. An old English word, now become obsolete. "And PILATE axide him, 'Art thou King of Jewis?' And Jhesus answeride and seide to him, 'Thou seist.' "— Wicliff's Bible, cited by BARTLETT.

Back and forth, instead of backward and forwards.

Back, instead of ago. A little while back.

Back down (*to*) instead of to recant.

Back out, instead of to retreat, or to fail to fulfil a promise; equivalent expressions are *to back water, to take the back track.*

9*

Backing and filling. Advancing and retreating.

Backward, instead of bashful, or modest.

Baggage. " The English," says BARTLETT, " appear to have discarded the word altogether, for the less appropriate term *luggage.*" I confess I do not see why it is less appropriate to the heavy trunks of which modern luggage chiefly consists.

Beast, instead of horse. Obsolete.

Beat — the beat of, instead of superior.

Beat out, instead of tired, or fatigued.

Beautiful, instead of excellent; as beautiful butter.

Beef, (*a*) instead of an ox.

Belongings, instead of attributes, garments, associations, or property.

Bestowment and *Bestowal.* Obsolete theological words.

Betterment, instead of improvement.

Bettermost, instead of the best.

Biddable, instead of manageable.

Big figure, (*on the*) instead of on a large scale.

Biggest, instead of greatest, or finest; as, she's the biggest kind of a singer.

Blow, (*to*) instead of to boast.

Blow out at, instead of to abuse.

Bluff off, (*to*). To deter, to put down, or repel.

Bone, (*to*) instead of to steal.

Bound, instead of determined or resolved. I'm bound to go.

Brown (*to do up*). To do anything to perfection.

Bub, bubby. Applied to small boys. From the German *Bube.*

Build, instead of to establish.

Bulger, instead of something extremely large.

Bully, instead of fine, or capital.

Burned up, instead of burned down.

By the name of. A man by the name of Smith. " An Englishman would say ' of the name of Smith,' except in such phrases as : ' He went by the name of Smith.' " — BARTLETT.

Bad, instead of ill ; as, I feel bad. Done bad.

Balance, instead of remainder.

Back out, (*to*) instead of to retreat.

Bogus, instead of counterfeit.

Banter, (*to*) instead of challenge.

Belittle, (*to*) instead of to make smaller.

Cannot, instead of can not.

Captivate, (*to*) instead of to take captive.

Conclude, instead of determine.

Connection. In this connection, instead of in connection with this subject.

County.   Instead of Westchester County we should say the County of Westchester.

Clear out, (*to*) instead of depart, or leave.

Clever does not mean good natured or well disposed, but dexterous, skilful, quick-witted, or intelligent.

Clip, instead of a sudden blow.

Cloud up, (*to*) instead of to grow cloudy.

Common.   As well as common, instead of as well as usual.

Conduct, (*to*) instead of to conduct oneself. " This vulgar expression has, with many others, been sanctioned by WEBSTER." — BARTLETT'S *Dictionary of Americanisms.*

Considerable, instead of much, or considerably.

Contemplate, (*to*) instead of to consider, to have in view, or to intend.

Corner, (*to*) instead of to get the advantage of any one.

Count, (*to*) instead of to reckon, suppose, or think.

Crowd, instead of company.

Cry, (*to*) instead of to publish the banns of marriage.

Cupalo, instead of cupola.

Converse together, (*to*) instead of to converse.

Cut round, (*to*) instead of to run about, or make a display.

Come, (*to*) instead of to go.

Cut under, (*to*) instead of to undersell.

Corporeal means having a body ; corporal, belonging or relating to the body.   We should say, corporal punishment, and, God is an incorporeal being.

Declension, or *declination,* instead of a refusal to accept.

Deed, (*to*) instead of to transfer by deed.

Deputize, (*to*) instead of to depute, to empower to act for another.

Dessert.   This word is applicable to the fruits and other delicacies brought on the table after the puddings and pies, but not to the puddings and pies themselves.

Dicker, (*to*) instead of to barter.

Difficulted, instead of perplexed.

Directly, instead of when, or as soon as.

Dirt.   This word is used in a too extended sense instead of earth, clay, or dust.

Dissipate (*to*).   To live idly or irregularly.

Do tell! instead of really ! or indeed !

Donation, instead of present.

Done, instead of did.

Don't, instead of does not.   *Don't* is a contraction for do not.

Dove, instead of dived.

Down upon.   Used to express enmity or dislike.

Down cellar, instead of down *in* the cellar.

Dragged out, instead of fatigued, òr exhausted.

Dreadful, instead of very.   " This, and the words
  awful, terrible, desperate, monstrous, are used by
  uneducated people for the purpose of giving emphasis to an expression."— BARTLETT.

Drinking.   Never say " he's a drinking man."

Driving at.   What are you driving at? instead of
  'what object have you in view?

Dump, instead of unload.

Egg, instead of to pelt with eggs.

Elect, instead of to prefer, to choose, to determine
  in favor of; as, they elected to submit; travellers
  will elect to go by the Northern route.

Elegant, for excellent, as applied, for instance, to
  articles of food; as, elegant pies.

Emptyings, for lees, or leaven.

Endorse, (*to*) instead of to approve, or confirm.

Eventuate, (*to*) instead of to happen, or to result in.

Experience.   Vulgarly used without an adjective,
  to describe religious trials and their result.

Experience religion, (*to,*) instead of to be con-
  verted.

Expect, (*to*) is only applicable to the anticipation of future events. It is vulgarly used for think, believe, or know.

Fair, instead of real, or genuine.

Fall, (*to*) instead of to fell a tree.

Fancy. This word is too generally used as an adjective ·to signify ornamental, fantastic, stylish, extraordinary, or choice; as, fancy prices, fancy houses, fancy women.

Fellowship (*to*). Vulgarly used as a verb.

Female. Incorrectly used to denote a person of the female sex. To speak of a woman simply as a female, is ridiculous.

Fetch up, (*to*) instead of to halt suddenly.

Fire away, instead of to begin.

First instead of one, or single. ·An absurd use of the word, as when one says, " I will not pay the first cent."

First rate, instead of superior.

Fix, (*to*) means to fasten, or make firm. One may fix a residence at New York; some men have no fixed opinions; you may fix a line to a hook; a preacher may fix the attention of his audience; and in chemistry, gold is a fixed body.

Fixed fact, instead of a positive or well established

fact. The invention of the phrase, according to Bartlett, is attributed to Caleb Cushing.

Fizzle, (to) instead of to fail, or to perform imper‐ fectly.

Forever, instead of for ever.

Flat broke, instead of entirely out of money.

Floor, (to have the) is the American term for to have possession of the house.

Flunk, instead of to fail, to retreat; as, to flunk out.

Flier, instead of a venture.

Fly. To fly around, instead of to stir about, or be active.

Folks, instead of people, or persons.

For, before the infinite particle to, has become very vulgar; as, I'd have you for to know.

Fore handed, instead of to be in good circumstances.

Foreigner. "Virginians call all other Americans *foreigners."* — BARTLETT.

Fork over — or up, instead of to pay.

Found, instead of fined.

Freshet, instead of flood, was once used in England, but is now confined as a word to the United States.

Funeralize, instead of to perform the clerical duties preparatory to a funeral

Funk, instead of an offensive smoke, smell, or dust.

Funk, (*to*) instead of to retreat, to resign, or to alarm.

Gale, instead of a state of excitement.

Garrison, instead of fort.

Gather, instead of to take up. One may gather apples, but not a stick.

Get, instead of to have; as, I have got no money. Inelegantly used to prevail on, or induce, or persuade. To get religion, instead of to become pious, is vulgar. So are, to get one's back up, get out! and to get round, instead of to get the better of.

Given name, instead of Christian name.

Go by, (*to*) instead of to call or stop at. A low Southern expression.

Go for, or *go in for*, (*to*) instead of to be in favor of.

Go it. As, to go it blind, to go it with a looseness, to go it strong, to go one's death, to go the big figure, or the whole figure.

Go off, (*to*) instead of to expire.

Go through the mill, (*to*) instead of to acquire experience.

Go under, (*to*) instead of to perish.

Going, instead of travelling; as the going is bad, it is bad going.

Gone, as in gone coon, gone goose.

Goner, instead of one who is lost.

Gone with, instead of become of. As, what is gone with him ?

Good. An incorrect use of this word may be heard in, he reads good; it does not run good. Very vulgar indeed is the phrase, " it is no good."

Gouge, instead of to cheat.

Governmental, instead of relating to government.

Grain, (*a*) instead of a little.

Grand, instead of very good, or excellent; as, it is a grand day.

Grant, (*to*) instead of to vouchsafe; as, grant to hear us.

Grass widow. Vulgar in any sense. In England it means an unmarried woman who has had a child. American editors, and even American ladies sometimes use this word unconscious of its real meaning.

Great, instead of distinguished, or excellent. Thus, he is a great Christian ; she is great at the piano.

Great big, instead of very large.

Green, instead of uncouth, raw, or inexperienced. It is, for example, vulgar to say, a green Fresh-man.

Grist, instead of a large number.

Guess, (*to*) means to conjecture, and not to believe, know, suppose, think, or imagine. It was once used by English writers in this positive sense, but is now vulgar and obselete.

Hack, instead of hackney coach. A hack is a livery stable horse.

Had have. A very low expression. Had we have known this.

Had not ought to, instead of ought not to.

Haint, instead of have not.

Hand, instead of adept, or proficient; as, you are a great hand at running.

Hand running, instead of consecutively.

Handsomely, instead of carefully, steadily, or correctly,

Hang. To get the hang of a thing, instead of becoming familiar with it. "He hadn't got the hang of the game."

Hang fire, instead of to delay, or to be impeded.

Hang around, instead of loiter about.

Hang out, instead of dwell.

Happen in, (*to*) instead of to happen to call in.

Hard case. Used to indicate a worthless fellow, or one who is hard to deal with.

Hard pushed, hard run, hard up, instead of hard pressed.

Haze, instead of to riot, to frolic, to urge or drive severely, to torment, or to annoy. .

Head off, instead of to intercept.

Heap, instead of many or much.

Heft, instead of weight, or to weigh.

Help, instead of servants.

Hide, instead of to beat.

High falutin, instead of high flown.

Hire. "Often improperly applied to renting a house. In good English, a house is rented, while a vehicle is hired." — BARTLETT.

Hitch, instead of entanglement or impediment.

Hold on, instead of to wait, or stop.

Hook, (*to*) instead of to steal.

Hook, (*on his own*) instead of on his own account.

Hooter. A corruption of iota; as, I don't care a hooter for him. .

Hopping mad, instead of very angry.

Horn (*in a*). Expressing dissent.

Horrors, instead of to be in low spirits. It is also used to indicate the peculiar state of mind which *succeeds* an attack of delirium tremens.

Horse, instead of man. Old hoss.

Hove, instead of heaved.

How? instead of what? or what did you say?

> " Do put your accents in the proper spot ;
> Don't — let me beg you — don't say *How?* for what? "
>
> — O. W. HOLMES.

How come? instead of how came it? how did it happen ?

Human, instead of human being. Very low.

Hung. " In England, beef is hung, gates are hung, and curtains are hung, but felons are *hanged.*" - REV. A. C. GEIKIE.

Hunk, instead of a large piece.

Hush up, dry up, and *shut up,* instead of to be silent.

Homely, instead of plain-featured or ugly.

Illy. A silly amplification of ill; as, I have been *illy* entreated.

In, instead of into; as, to get in the stage, to come in town.

Independent fortune. A man may be rendered independent by a fortune, but the fortune can hardly become independent of a possessor.

Institution. A word vaguely applied to any prevalent practice or thing.

Item, instead of information.

Job, instead of thrust.

Jag. Used to express a parcel, or load; also a
. habit adopted for a time, as he is on a moral jag;
also for intoxication.

Japonicadom, instead of the fashionable class of
society.

Jew, (*to*) instead of to cheat.

Jessie, (*to give*) instead of to treat severely.

Jump, (*from the*) instead of from the beginning.

Keel over, instead of to be prostrated, or die.

Keep, instead of food, subsistence, keeping.

Keep a stiff upper lip, instead of to keep up one's
courage, to continue firm.

Keep company, (*to*) instead of to court, or make
love.

Keeping-room, instead of the sitting-room or parlor.

Kesouse, keswap, keswack, to express dipping, or
falling into water.

Kerslap. Used to indicate a flat fall.

Kick up a row, or *dust*, instead of to create a dis-
turbance.

Kill, (*to*) instead of to defeat, in politics.

Kind of, instead of in a manner, or as it were.

Kink, instead of an accidental knot or twist. Also
used incorrectly for a fanciful notion.

Knock, instead of astonish or overwhelm; as that knocks me.

Knock about, or *round,* (*to,*) instead of to go about.

Larrup, instead of beat.

Luther, instead of beat.

Law, (*to*) instead of to go to law.

Lay, instead of to lie; as, he laid down, instead of he lay down to sleep; or, "the land lays well."

Lay. Terms of a bargain, price. Also, the occupation or employment of any one.

Lengthy, lengthily, instead of having length, long; as, a lengthy oration.

Let be, (*to*) instead of to let alone; as, let me be!

Let on, instead of to mention, to disclose.

Let out, instead of to begin narrating.

Let slide, rip, went, travel, circulate, agitate, drive, fly, instead of to let go.

Let up, instead of a release or relief.

Levee, "in the United States is often applied to ceremonious receptions given by official personages, whether in the morning or evening. In England the word is restricted to morning receptions."— APPLETON'S *Cyclopædia.* As the word is of French origin, from *levér,* to rise, and was at first applied to the concourse of people who attended the rising of a prince from bed, it will be seen that the American application of the word to an *evening* reception is very absurd.

Licks, instead of efforts, strokes, or exertion.

Lickety split, instead of headlong, very fast.

Liefer, liever, liefs, lieves, instead of more willingly, or rather.

Lift,, instead of aid, help, or assistance. Also, improperly used for a ride.

Like, instead of as, or as if, or as though. A very vulgar and very common expression. Like I always do. He drank like he was used to it.

Likely, instead of intelligent, promising, or able. Also used to signify beauty.

Limb. A silly and affected expression for leg.

Liquor, liquor up, instead of to take a dram.

Little end o· the horn. Applied, like the Italian word *fiasco,* (or bottle) to a failure.

Loafer. Originally applied to a pilferer, and subsequently to a vagabond.

Loan, (to) instead of to lend.

Locate, (to) instead of to settle in.

Looseness, instead of freedom. A perfect looseness.

Love, (to) instead of to like. "I *love* apple pie,"

said a lady. "You could say no more for your child or husband," replied an old bachelor who was present.

Lummocks, instead of a heavy, stupid fellow.

Mad, instead of very angry. "A low word." — PICKERING.

Mail, instead of post. Mail is properly the bag in which the letters are carried.

Make a raise, (*to*) instead of to obtain.

Make tracks, instead of to go or to run.

Marm, or *Ma'am*, instead of Mamma, or mother. My Ma'am says so.

Mate, or match. Used in speaking of shoes or gloves, for fellow.

Mean, instead of means.

Mean, instead of poor, base, or worthless.

Meeting, meeting-house, instead of a place of worship, or church.

Middling, instead of tolerably.

Middling interest, instead of the middle class.

Midst. In our midst, instead of among us. There is, properly, no such noun as midst. The expression is used by eminent authors, but is become vulgar.

Mighty, instead of very; as, mighty nice.

Mind, (*to*) instead of to recollect, remember. Also, instead of to watch, or take care of.

Missing. Among the missing, instead of absent.

Mistake. And no mistake, instead of sure.

Mixed up, instead of confused, promiscuous.

Monstrous, instead of very, or exceedingly.

More, most, instead of the regular comparative and superlative terminations. " A more full vocabulary." — See the preface to WORCESTER's *Dictionary*, 1856. More fond of cards.

Most, instead of almost.

Move, instead of to remove, or to change one's residence.

Much. Used in praise or dispraise. I e is not much of a man.

Mungy, instead of false or feigned. From "r ongrel."

Muss, instead of a quarrel.

Muss, (*to*) instead of to disarrange, to disorder.

Nary, instead of ne'er a. " Did you see Ary Scheffer in Paris?" " Nary Scheffer," was the reply

Narrate. Used by good authority, but of doubtful excellence. *Norate* is certainly vulgar.

Nigh unto, u, in, instead of nearly, or almost.

Necessitate, instead of to be obliged, or compelled.

Nimshi, instead of a foolish fellow.

Nip and tuck, instead of equal.

No not. Some people absurdly use double negatives; as, I wont no-how; it aint, neither; I aint got none.

No-account, instead of worthless. A no-account fellow.

No-how, instead of by no means.

Nothing else. A vulgar affirmation. It aint nothing else.

Notions, instead of small wares, or trifles.

Notional, instead of whimsical.

Nub, instead of point, or significance.

Obliged to be, instead of must be.

Obligated, instead of to compel.

Odd stick, or *odd fish,* instead of eccentric person.

Of. Many people in using the verbs to smell, feel, to taste, supply the preposition of; as, to smell of it.

Off the handle. To fly off the handle, instead of to fly into a passion. *To go off the handle,* instead of to die.

Offish, instead of distant.

Off-set, (*to*) instead of set-off.

Obnoxious, instead of offensive

Older-est, instead of elder, eldest.

Old man, old gentleman, instead of father.

On. He lives on a street, instead of in a street
passage on a steamboat.

On it, instead of implicated, interested in it, or be-
lieving in it.

On hand, instead of at hand, present.

Once and again, instead of occasionally.

On the coast, instead of near, close at hand.

Oncet, (pronounced *wunst,*) and *twicet,* or *twist,*
for once and twice.   A Saxon form.

Onto, instead of on, or to.

On yesterday, instead of yesterday.

Ought.   Wrongly used in hadn't ought, had ought
to, don't ought.

Ourn, instead of ours.

Over, instead of under, (or sometimes above) ; as,
he writes over the signature of Caius.

Over-run, instead of to run over.

Overture, instead of to propose.

Owdacious, instead of audacious.

Partly, instead of nearly, or almost.   His house is
partly opposite to mine.

Patentable, instead of that may be patented.

Peaked instead of thin, or emaciated.

Peg out, instead of die.

Pending, instead of during. A common affectation. Pending the conversation. Pending the session.

Pesky, peskily, instead of annoying.

Pile, instead of money amassed, or fortune.

Place, instead of to identify with one's birth-place or home. I can't place him.

Plaguy, plaguy sight, instead of very, extremely, or very much.

Plank, instead of to lay, or put down.

Play actor, instead of actor.

Played out, instead of exhausted.

Plead, instead of pleaded.

Plum, instead of direct, or straight. He looked me plum in the face.

Poke fun, (*to*) instead of to joke, to ridicule.

Pokerish, instead of frightful, or fearful.

Poky, instead of stupid.

Pond. " Used in America to signify a body of water smaller than a lake, with either natural or artificial banks. In England the word pond implies that the water is confined by an artificial bank." -- APPLETON'S *Cyclopædia.*

Pony up, instead of to pay over.

Posted up, instead of fully informed.

Powerful, instead of very, or exceedingly

Prayerful and *prayerfully,* instead of devout cr devoutly; using prayer, or disposed to pray.

Prayerfulness, Prayerlessness. The use or neglect of prayer,

Predicated upon, instead of founded upon basis or data. A word of very doubtful purity.

Pretty considerable, middling, instead of tolerable.

Preventative, instead of preventive.

Primp up. Dressed up stylishly.

Profanity. English writers generally use the word profaneness.

Professor, instead of one who is professedly religious. As a title, the word is incorrectly applied except to a teacher in an university or college.

Proper, instead of very; as, proper frightened.

Proud, instead of glad. He is proud to know.

Proud, instead of honor. Sir, you do me proud.

Pucker (in a). Fright, agitation.

Pull foot pull it, instead of to walk fast, or run.

Put. Stay put, instead of to remain in order.

Put, put out, put off. To decamp.

Put the licks in. To exert oneself.

Put through, instead of to accomplish, or conclude.

Quite, instead of very; as, it is quite cold.

Rail, (*to*) instead of to travel by rail.

Raise a racket, raise Cain, (*to*) instead of to make a noise.

Rake down. To reduce, to mortify.

Reckon, instead of to think or imagine.

Reliable, instead of trustworthy.

Rehash, instead of repetition.

Remind, instead of remember.

Renewedly, instead of anew, again, once more.

Rendition, instead of rendering.

Re-open. To open again. A word of doubtful correctness.

Result, (*to*) instead of to decree, or to decide.

Resurrect, instead of to reanimate.

Retiracy, instead of retirement, or a competency.

Rich, instead of entertaining or amusing.

Ride, instead of to carry or transport. In England the word is restricted by writers of the present day, to going on horseback.

Rights (*to*), *right away, right off,* instead of directly, or at once.

Right smart, instead of large, or great.

Rile. To make angry. Provincial in England.

Rise, rising, instead of more. A thousand and the rise. Rising a thousand dollars.

Rocks, instead of money, or stones.

Room, instead of to occupy a room, or to lodge.

Rope in, instead of to decoy, or to inveigle.

Rounds. Going the rounds of the papers is called an Americanism in England.

Rowdy, instead of a riotous, turbulent fellow.

Row up, instead of to punish with words, or to rebuke.

Run, run upon, instead of to quiz.

Run one's face, instead of to get credit by a good personal appearance.

Run to the ground, instead of to carry to excess.

Rush, instead of spirit, or energy.

River. English say " the river Thames." Americans say, " the Ohio river."

Safe, instead of sure, certain.

Sauce, instead of culinary vegetables and roots.

Save, instead of to make sure, or to kill.

Saw, instead of joke, or trick. To run a saw on him.

Scallawag, instead of vile fellow, or scamp.

Scare up, instead of to find.

Scary, instead of easily scared.

School Ma'am, instead of school mistress or teacher

Scooped him in, instead of inveigled.

Scoot, instead of to walk fast.

Scratch, (*no great*) instead of value.

Scrawny, instead of spare, cr bony.

Scrimp, instead of scanty.   Of doubtful propriety

Scrouge, instead of to crowd.

Scrumptious, instead of scrupulous.

Scup, instead of swing.

Scurry, instead of to scour, to run in haste.

Scurse, *Scuss*, instead of scarce.

Seen, instead of saw.

Serious, instead of religious.

Serve up, (*to*) instead of to expose to ridicule.

Set, instead of obstinate ; as, a set man.

Set, instead of to fix, or to obstruct, or to stop.

Settle, (*to*) instead of ordained.   He settled in the
  ministry very young.

Shack, instead of a vagabond.

Shake a stick at.   A vulgar comparative.

Shanghai, instead of fop.

Shew, (pronounced *shoo*), instead of showed.   I
  shew him the difference.   A very vulgar error.

Shimmy, instead of chemise.

Shin round. To fly about.

Shindy, instead of a riot, a liking, or fancy.

Shine. Show, display. She cut a shine. Also, to succeed with. He shines up to her.

Shingle, instead of sign.

Shinplaster. A small bank-note.

Shote. A worthless fellow.

Shyster. A low lawyer. A word of filthy German origin, and utterly unfit to use.

Sick. Sickness is only applicable to nausea, or sickness at the stomach. It is the common American word for ill.

Sight. A great many, a deal.

Skeary, instead of scary.

Skedaddle, (to) instead of to escape, or to depart.

Skimped, instead of scanty.

Slantendicular. Aslant.

Slick up, (to) instead of to make fine.

Slimsy, instead of flimsy.

Slink. A sneaking fellow.

Slipe. A distance.

Slops. To run away, to evade.

Smart. In America, smart is used as signifying quick, or shrewd. In England, it usually has the meaning of showy.

Smart chance, instead of a good opportunity. Like it, we have a smart piece, and a smart sprinkle.

Smouch, (*to*) instead of to cheat. A Jew, in England is vulgarly called a smouch.

Snake (*to*). To crawl like a snake. To cunningly advance towards one.

Snarl, instead of an entangled quarrel.

Snippy, *snippish*, instead of finical, or conceited.

So, instead of such. " Prof. W——, who has acquired *so* high distinction."— BARTLETT.

Sockdolloger. A final argument, or blow.

Sock. Sock down. To pay money down.

Soft sodder, soap. Flattery, soft persuasion.

Some. Of some account, famous. Of the same application, some pumpkins.

Soon, instead of early. *Sooner, very soon*, instead of at once, or directly, or soon.

Sozzle. To immerse. To move while dipping.

Sound on the goose. True, staunch.

Span of horses. An Americanism applied to a pair, and always implies resembance. "The word signifies, properly, the same as yoke, when applied to horned cattle."— BARTLETT.

Spark (*to*). To court.

Spat. A slap, a quarrel.

Specie, instead of species.   Specie is hard money.

Spell.   A turn of work.   A time, an interval.

Spit curl.   A lock of hair curled upon the temple

Split.   A division, dissension.   Also, a rapid pace; as, full split.   To inform on.

Splurge.   A blustering demonstration, a swagger, a dash.

Spoopsy   A silly fellow.

Sposh.   Mud, or snow and water.

Spread oneself (*to*).   To make great efforts.

Spread eagle.   Applied to vulgar rant and bombast. It is rapidly becoming a very contemptuous term.

Spree (*to*).   To riot, and get drunk.

Sprouts (*a course of*).   A severe initiation.   The term is derived from the Thompsonian practice. " Vegetable."

Spry.   Lively, active.   Provincial in England.

Spunk.   Spirit, vivacity.   A very vulgar word.

Squawk, instead of a failure.

Squiggle.   To wriggle.

Squirt.   A coxcomb.   A vulgar word.

Squush.   To crush.

Stag.   Where only male persons are assembled.   A stag party.

Stamping ground.   A favorite and familiar place of resort.

Stand. The situation ot a place of business.

Stand treat (*to*). To pay for a treat.

Stave along. To hurry onward.

Steamboat. A dashing, go-ahead character.

Steep, or tall. Great, magnificent.

Stick (*to*). To impose upon, to render liable.

Stop, (*to*) instead of to stay for a time.

Stout, instead of obstinate.

Straight out. Downright, candid.

Strapped. Wanting money. ·

Streaked, streaky, instead of alarmed.

Streak it (*to*). To run fast.

Stretch (*on a*). Continuously.

String. A row, a number.

Stripe. Pattern, sort.

Stuffy. Angry, obstinate, sulky.

Stump (*to*). To challenge. To confound.

Suck in (*to*). To deceive. A low word.

Sucker. A mean fellow. A drunkard. One who imposes or preys on others.

Suspicion, (*to*) instead of to suspect.

Swap, swop, instead of barter, or exchange.

Systemize, (*to*) instead of to systematize. "A word rarely used by good writers."—WORCESTER

Take to do (*to*).   To take to task.   To reprove.

'Taint, instead of it is not.

Take the back track (*to*).   To recede.

Take the rag off (*to*).   To surpass.

Take on (*to*).   To grieve, mourn.

Talk, (*a*) instead of conversation, or discussion.

Tall, instead of fine, splendid, or grand.

Tavern.   In England, only food or drink, and not lodging, is provided at a tavern.

Tax, instead of charge.   What do you tax us for it?

Team.   A person of energy.   He is a whole team.

Teetotally.   Entirely, totally.

Tell, instead of report.   A compliment; as, I've a tell for you.

Tell on (*to*).   To tell of, to tell about.   ·

Tend, instead of attend, or wait.

The.   Vulgarly used before the names of diseases; as, he died of the cholera.   Many persons say, he speaks the French, or the German.   The correct mode of expression would be, he speaks French, or the French language.

There.   Used for the future tense with I am; as, I'm there.

This here, and *that there,* for this, and that.

Those sort of things, instead of that sort of things.

Throw in. To contribute.

Thundering, instead of very.

Tie to, instead of to trust, to rely on.

Tight, instead of tipsy.

Tight place — squeeze, instead of a difficulty.

To, instead of in, or at. He is to home.

Toe the mark (to). To fulfil obligations.

Top notch. The highest point.

Tote, instead of to carry.

Touch. No touch to it. Not to be compared to it.

Trainers, training. The militia when assembled for exercise.

Travel, instead of to depart.

Try on, instead of to try.

Tuckered out. Fatigued, exhausted.

Tuck, for took.

Transient. A transient boarder. Not used in this sense in England.

Transpire, instead of to happen, or to be done.

Uncommon, instead of uncommonly.

Up to the hub. To the extreme.

Upper ten-thousand (the). A silly slang term for the higher circles of society.

Use up, (to) instead of to exhaust.

Vamose. (Let us go. Spanish.) Used instead of depart, be off. To vamose the ranch.

Vum, (*I*) instead of I vow, or declare.

Wake up the wrong passenger (*to*). To make a mistake as to an individual.

Walk chalk. To walk straight.

Walk into (*to*). To take the advantage of. To punish, or treat severely.

Walking papers. Orders to leave · dismissal.

Wallop (*to*). To beat.

Wamble cropt. Depressed; humiliated.

Wa'nt, instead of was not, and were not.

Want to know? Do tell? Very vulgar interjections.

Ways. Way, distance, space.

Ways. *No two ways about it,* instead of the fact is just so.

Well to do — to live, instead of well off.

Went. You should have went, instead of you should have gone.

Whap over (*to*). To knock over.

Whapper, whopper. Anything uncommonly large.

What for a. What for a man is that? instead of what kind of a man is that?

Which, instead of what, who, he, they. Also very vulgarly used as a pleonasm. Mr. Brown which he said he would go.

While, instead of till, or until. Stay while I come.

Whittled down to. Reduced.

Whole heap. Many, all, several, much.

Whole souled. Noble minded. "A phrase in great favor with persons fond of fine talking."— BART-LETT.

Whole team. A general compliment, implying the possession of many powers.

Wide awake, instead of on the alert.

Wilt down (to). To depress.

Wind up, instead of to silence; to settle.

Wire edge. The edge removed in the form of a strip when sharpening a tool. It is incorrectly used to signify a sharp, or fine edge.

Wool over the eyes (to draw the). To impose on.

Worryment. Trouble, anxiety.

Worst kind of, instead of in the worst or severest manner.

Wrath. Like all wrath, instead of violently.

Wrathy, instead of angry.

Yank. A jerk. To yank, to bring forth; pull out; manipulate.

Yellow cover. Applied to chcap and vulgar litera-
turc; so called first in 1840, from the twenty-five
cent editions of Paul de Kock's novels, and similar
works.

Yourn, instead of yours, or your own.

THE END.

NEW BOOKS

And New Editions Recently Issued by
CARLETON, Publisher, New York,

Madison Square, corner Fifth Av. and Broadway.]

N. B.—THE PUBLISHERS, upon receipt of the price in advance, will send any of the following Books by mail, POSTAGE FREE, to any part of the United States. This convenient and very safe mode may be adopted when the neighboring Book sellers are not supplied with the desired work. State name and address in full.

Marion Harland's Works.

ALONE.—	. . A novel. . .	12mo. cloth,	$1.50
HIDDEN PATH.—	. do. . .	do.	$1.50
MOSS SIDE.—	. do. . .	do.	$1.50
NEMESIS.—	. . do. . .	do.	$1.50
MIRIAM.—	. . do. . .	do.	$1.50
AT LAST.—	do. *Just Published.*		$1.50
HELEN GARDNER'S WEDDING-DAY.—	. . . do.		$1.50
SUNNYBANK.—	. do. . .	do.	$1.50
HUSBANDS AND HOMES.—	do. . .	do.	$1.50
RUBY'S HUSBAND.—	do. . .	do.	$1.50
PHEMIE'S TEMPTATION.—		do.	$1.50

Miss Muloch.

JOHN HALIFAX.—A novel. With illustration.	12mo. cloth,	$1.75
A LIFE FOR A LIFE.—	. do.	do.	$1.75

Charlotte Bronte (Currer Bell).

JANE EYRE.—A novel. With illustration.	12mo. cloth,	$1.75
THE PROFESSOR.— do. . do. .	do.	$1.75
SHIRLEY.— . do. . do. .	do.	$1.75
VILLETTE.— . do. . do. .	do.	$1.75

Hand-Books of Society.

THE HABITS OF GOOD SOCIETY; thoughts, hints, and anecdotes, concerning nice points of taste, good manners, and the art of making oneself agreeable. . . 12mo. cloth, $1.75

THE ART OF CONVERSATION.—A sensible and instructive work, that ought to be in the hands of every one who wishes to be either an agreeable talker or listener. 12mo. cloth, $1.50

ARTS OF WRITING, READING, AND SPEAKING.—An excellent book for self-instruction and improvement. 12mo. cloth, $1.50

HAND-BOOKS OF SOCIETY.—The above three choice volumes bound in extra style, full gilt ornamental back, uniform in appearance, and in a handsome box. . . . $5.00

Mrs. Mary J. Holmes' Works.

'LENA RIVERS.— . . .	A novel. 12mo. cloth,	$1.50
DARKNESS AND DAYLIGHT.— .	do. . do. .	$1.50
TEMPEST AND SUNSHINE.— .	do. . do. .	$1.50
MARIAN GREY.— . . .	do. . do. .	$1.50
MEADOW BROOK.— . . .	do. . do. .	$1 50
ENGLISH ORPHANS.— .	do. . do. .	$1.50
DORA DEANE.— . . .	do. . do. .	$1 50
COUSIN MAUDE.— . . .	do. . do. .	$1 50
HOMESTEAD ON THE HILLSIDE.—	do. . do. .	$1.50
HUGH WORTHINGTON.— . .	do. . do. .	$1.50
THE CAMERON PRIDE.— . .	do. . do. .	$1.50
ROSE MATHER.— . . .	do. . do. .	$1.50
ETHELYN'S MISTAKE.—*Just Published.* do. .	do. .	$1.50

Miss Augusta J. Evans.

BEULAH.—A novel of great power. .	12mo. cloth,	$1.75
MACARIA.— · do. do. .	do. .	$1.75
ST. ELMO.— do. do.	do. .	$2.00
VASHTI.— do. do. *Just Published.*	do .	$2.00

Victor Hugo.

LES MISÉRABLES.—The celebrated novel. One large 8vo volume, paper covers, $2.00 ; . . . cloth bound, $2.50
LES MISÉRABLES.—Spanish. Two vols., paper, $4.00 ; cl., $5.00

Mrs. A. P. Hill.

MRS. HILL'S NEW COOKERY BOOK, and receipts. . . $2.00

Algernon Charles Swinburne.

LAUS VENERIS, AND OTHER POEMS.— . 12mo. cloth, $1.75

Captain Mayne Reid's Works—Illustrated.

THE SCALP HUNTERS.—	A romance.	12mo. cloth, $1.50
THE RIFLE RANGERS.— .	do. .	do. . $1.50
THE TIGER HUNTER.— .	do. .	do. . $1.50
OSCEOLA, THE SEMINOLE.— .	do. .	do. . $1.50
THE WAR TRAIL.— . .	do. .	do . $1.50
THE HUNTER'S FEAST.— .	do. .	do. . $1.50
RANGERS AND REGULATORS.—	do. .	do. . $1.50
THE WHITE CHIEF.— . .	do. .	do. . $1 50
THE QUADROON.— . .	do. .	do. . $1 50
THE WILD HUNTRESS.— .	do	do. . $1 50
THE WOOD RANGERS.— .	do. .	do. . $1.50
WILD LIFE.— . . .	do. .	do. . $1 50
THE MAROON.— . . .	do. .	do. . $1 50
LOST LEONORE.— . .	do. .	do. . $1.50
THE HEADLESS HORSEMAN.—	do. .	do. . $1.50
THE WHITE GAUNTLET.— *Just Published.*		do. . $1.50

A. S. Roe's Works.

A LONG LOOK AHEAD.—	A novel.	12mo. cloth,	$1.50
TO LOVE AND TO BE LOVED.—	do.	do.	$1.50
TIME AND TIDE.—	do.	do.	$1.50
I'VE BEEN THINKING.—	do.	do.	$1.50
THE STAR AND THE CLOUD.—	do.	do.	$1.50
TRUE TO THE LAST.—	do.	do.	$1.50
HOW COULD HE HELP IT ?—	do.	do.	$1.50
LIKE AND UNLIKE.—	do.	do.	$1.50
LOOKING AROUND.—	do.	do.	$1.50
WOMAN OUR ANGEL.—	do.	do.	$1.50
THE CLOUD ON THE HEART.—*Just published.*	do.	$1.50

Richard B. Kimball.

WAS HE SUCCESSFUL ?—	A novel.	12mo. cloth,	$1.75
UNDERCURRENTS.—	do.	do.	$1.75
SAINT LEGER.—	do.	do.	$1.75
ROMANCE OF STUDENT LIFE.—do.	do.	$1.75
IN THE TROPICS.—	do.	do.	$1.75
HENRY POWERS, Banker.	do.	do.	$1.75
TO-DAY.—A novel. *Just published.*	do.	$1.75

Joseph Rodman Drake.

THE CULPRIT FAY.—A faery poem, with 100 illustrations. $2.00
DO. Superbly bound in turkey morocco. $5.00

"Brick" Pomeroy.

SENSE.—An illustrated vol. of fireside musings. 12mo. cl., $1.50
NONSENSE.— do. do. comic sketches. do. $1.50
OUR SATURDAY NIGHTS. do. pathos and sentiment. $1.50

Comic Books—Illustrated.

ARTEMUS WARD,	His Book.—Letters, etc.	12mo. cl.,	$1.50
DO.	His Travels—Mormons, etc.	do.	$1.50
DO.	In London.—Punch Letters.	do.	$1.50
DO.	His Panorama and Lecture.	do.	$1.50
DO.	Sandwiches for Railroad.		25
JOSH BILLINGS ON ICE, and other things.—	12mo. cl.,	$1.50
DO.	His Book of Proverbs, etc.	do.	$1.50
DO.	Farmer's Allmanax. *Just published.*	.25
FANNY FERN.—Folly as it Flies.		$1.50
DO.	Gingersnaps		$1.50
VERDANT GREEN.—A racy English college story. 12mo. cl.,	$1.50
CONDENSED NOVELS, ETC.—By F. Bret Harte.	do.	$1.50
MILES O'REILLY.—His Book of Adventures.	do.	$1.50
ORPHEUS C. KERR.—Kerr Papers, 3 vols.	do.	$1.50
DO.	Avery Glibun. A novel.		$2.00
DO.	Smoked Glass.	12mo. cl.,	$1.50

Children's Books—Illustrated.

THE ART OF AMUSING.—With 150 illustrations. 12mo. cl., $1.50
FRIENDLY COUNSEL FOR GIRLS.—A charming book. do. $1.50
THE CHRISTMAS FONT.—By Mary J. Holmes.   do. $1.00
ROBINSON CRUSOE.—A Complete edition.   .   do. $1.50
LOUIE'S LAST TERM.—By author "Rutledge."   do. $1.75
BOUNDHEARTS, and other stories.—   do.   .   do. $1.75
PASTIMES WITH MY LITTLE FRIENDS.—   .   .   do. $1.50
WILL-O'-THE-WISP.—From the German.   .   do. $1.50

M. Michelet's Remarkable Works.

LOVE (L'AMOUR).—Translated from the French. 12mo. cl., $1.50
WOMAN (LA FEMME).—   .   do.   .   .   do. $1.50

Ernest Renan.

THE LIFE OF JESUS.—Translated from the French. 12mo.cl., $1.75
THE APOSTLES.—   .   .   do.   .   .   do. $1.75
SAINT PAUL.—   .   .   do.   .   .   do. $1.75

Popular Italian Novels.

DOCTOR ANTONIO.—A love story. By Ruffini. 12mo. cl., $1.75
BEATRICE CENCI.—By Guerrazzi, with portrait.   do. $1.75

Rev. John Cumming, D.D., of London.

THE GREAT TRIBULATION.—Two series.   12mo. cloth, $1.50
THE GREAT PREPARATION.—   do.   .   do. $1.50
THE GREAT CONSUMMATION.   do.   .   do. $1.50
THE LAST WARNING CRY.—   .   .   do. $1.50

Mrs. Ritchie (Anna Cora Mowatt).

FAIRY FINGERS.—A capital new novel.   .   12mo. cloth, $1.75
THE MUTE SINGER.—   do.   .   do. $1.75
THE CLERGYMAN'S WIFE—and other stories.   do. $1.75

T. S. Arthur's New Works.

LIGHT ON SHADOWED PATHS.—A novel.   12mo. cloth, $1.50
OUT IN THE WORLD.—   .   do.   .   .   do. $1.50

WHAT CAME AFTERWARDS.—   do.   .   .   do. $1 50
OUR NEIGHBORS.—   .   do.   .   .   do. $1 50

Geo. W. Carleton.

OUR ARTIST IN CUBA.—With 50 comic illustrations.   . $1.50
UR ARTIST IN PERU.—   do.   do.   .   . $1.50
OUR ARTIST IN AFRICA.—(*In press*)   do.   . $1.50

John Esten Cooke.

FAIRFAX.—   A brilliant new novel. .   12mo. cloth, $1.50
HILT TO HILT.—   do.   .   .   .   do. $1.50
HAMMER AND RAPIER.—   do.   .   .   do. $1.50
OUT OF THE FOAM.—   do.   *In press.*   do. $1.50

How to Make Money

AND HOW TO KEEP IT.—A practical, readable book, that ought to be in the hands of every person who wishes to earn money or to keep what he has.   One of the best books ever published.   By Thomas A. Davies.   12mo. cloth, $1.5c

J. Cordy Jeaffreson.

A BOOK ABOUT LAWYERS.—A collection of interesting anec·dotes and incidents connected with the most distinguished members of the Legal Profession.   .   12mo. cloth, $2.00

Fred. Saunders.

WOMAN, LOVE, AND MARRIAGE.—A charming volume about three most fascinating topics.   .   .   12mo. cloth, $1.50

Edmund Kirke.

AMONG THE PINES.—Or Life in the South.   12mo. cloth, $1.50
MY SOUTHERN FRIENDS.—   do.   .   .   do. $1.50
DOWN IN TENNESSEE.—   do.   .   .   do. $1.50
ADRIFT IN DIXIE.—   do.   .   .   do. $1.50
AMONG THE GUERILLAS.—   do.   .   .   do. $1.50

Charles Reade.

THE CLOISTER AND THE HEARTH.—A magnificent new novel— the best this author ever wrote.   .   8vo. cloth, $2.00

The Opera.

TALES FROM THE OPERAS.—A collection of clever stories, based upon the plots of all the famous operas. 12mo. cloth, $1.50

Robert B. Roosevelt.

THE GAME-FISH OF THE NORTH.—Illustrated. 12mo. cloth, $2.00
SUPERIOR FISHING.—   do.   do. $2.00
THE GAME-BIRDS OF THE NORTH.—   .   . do. $2.00

By the Author of "Rutledge."

RUTLEDGE.—A deeply interesting novel.   12mo. cloth, $1.75
THE SUTHERLANDS.—   do.   .   .   do.   . $1.75
FRANK WARRINGTON.—   do.   .   .   do.   . $1.75
ST. PHILIP'S.—   do.   .   .   do.   . $1.75
LOUIE'S LAST TERM AT ST. MARY'S.—   .   do.   . $1.75
ROUNDHEARTS AND OTHER STORIES.—For children. do.   . $1.75
A ROSARY FOR LENT.—Devotional Readings.   do.   . $1.75

Love in Letters.

A collection of piquant love-letters.   .   12mo. cloth, $2.00

Dr. J. J. Craven.

THE PRISON-LIFE OF JEFFERSON DAVIS.— .   12mo. cloth, $2.00

Walter Barrett, Clerk.

THE OLD MERCHANTS OF NEW YORK.—   Five vols. cloth,$10.

H. T. Sperry.

COUNTRY LOVE vs. CITY FLIRTATION.—   .   12mo. cloth, $2 00

Miscellaneous Works.

CHRIS AND OTHO.—A novel by Mrs. Julie P. Smith. .	$1 75
CROWN JEWELS.— do. Mrs. Emma L. Moffett.	$1 75
ADRIFT WITH A VENGEANCE.— Kinahan Cornwallis. .	$1.50
THE FRANCO-PRUSSIAN WAR IN 1870.—By W. D. Landon.	
DREAM MUSIC.—Poems by Frederic Rowland Marvin. .	$1.50
RAMBLES IN CUBA.—By an American Lady. . .	$1.50
BEHIND THE SCENES, in the White House.—Keckley. .	$2.00
YACHTMAN'S PRIMER.—For Amateur Sailors.—Warren.	50
RURAL ARCHITECTURE.—By M. Field. With illustrations.	$2.00
TREATISE ON DEAFNESS.—By Dr. E. B. Lighthill. . .	$1.50
WOMEN AND THEATRES.—A new book, by Olive Logan.	$1.50
WARWICK.—A new novel by Mansfield Tracy Walworth.	$1.75
SIBYL HUNTINGTON.—A novel by Mrs. J. C. R. Dorr. .	$1.75
LIVING WRITERS OF THE SOUTH.—By Prof. Davidson. .	$2.00
STRANGE VISITORS.—A book from the Spirit World. .	$1.50
UP BROADWAY, and its Sequel.—A story by Eleanor Kirk.	$1.50
MILITARY RECORD, of Appointments in the U.S. Army.	$5.00
HONOR BRIGHT.—A new American novel. . . .	$1.50
MALBROOK.— do. do. do. . . .	$1.50
GUILTY OR NOT GUILTY.— do. do. . . .	$1.75
ROBERT GREATHOUSE.—A new novel by John F. Swift .	$2.00
THE GOLDEN CROSS, and poems by Irving Van Wart, jr.	$1.50
ATHALIAH.—A new novel by Joseph H. Greene, jr. .	$1.75
REGINA, and other poems.—By Eliza Cruger. . .	$1.50
THE WICKEDEST WOMAN IN NEW YORK.—By C. H. Webb.	50
MONTALBAN.—A new American novel. . . .	$1.75
MADEMOISELLE MERQUEM.—A novel by George Sand. .	$1.75
THE IMPENDING CRISIS OF THE SOUTH.—By H. R. Helper.	$2.00
NOJOQUE—A Question for a Continent.— do. .	$2.00
PARIS IN 1867.—By Henry Morford.	$1.75
THE BISHOP'S SON.—A novel by Alice Cary. . .	$1.75
CRUISE OF THE ALABAMA AND SUMTER.—By Capt. Semmes.	$1.50
HELEN COURTENAY.—A novel, author " Vernon Grove."	$1.75
SOUVENIRS OF TRAVEL.—By Madame Octavia W. LeVert.	$2.00
VANQUISHED.—A novel by Agnes Leonard. . .	$1.75
WILL-O'-THE-WISP.—A child's book, from the German .	$1.50
FOUR OAKS.—A novel by Kamba Thorpe. . . .	$1.75
THE CHRISTMAS FONT.—A child's book, by M. J. Holmes.	$1.00
POEMS, BY SARAH T. BOLTON.	$1.50
MARY BRANDEGEE—A novel by Cuyler Pine. . .	$1.75
RENSHAWE.— do. do. . . .	$1.75
MOUNT CALVARY.—By Matthew Hale Smith. . .	$2.00
PROMETHEUS IN ATLANTIS.—A prophecy. . . .	$2.00
TITAN AGONISTES.—An American novel. . . .	$2.00

www.ingramcontent.com/pod-product-compliance
Lightning Source LLC
Chambersburg PA
CBHW020114030726
47498CB00006B/2095